BY SPECIAL APPOINTMENT TO
H.R.H. THE DUKE OF EDINBURGH.

POINTMENT.

LORS.

THE QUEEN.

POOLE & Cº.

ss "ELOOP" LONDON)

SAVILE ROW, W.

, CLIFFORD STREET, W.

APPOINTMENT TO

OF BRAZIL.

HE BELGIANS.

OF SPAIN.

F DENMARK.

F PORTUGAL.

BY SPECIAL APPOINTMENT TO
HIS MAJESTY THE EMPEROR OF THE FRENCH.

EMPEROR OF RUSSIA.

H.R.H. PRINCE CHRISTIAN.

THE KING OF ITALY.

H. H. DUKE OF TECK.

H.R.H. THE PRINCE OF ORANGE.

SHAH OF PERSIA.

HENRY POOLE

Founders of Savile Row

The Making of a Legend

HENRY POOLE

Founders of Savile Row

The Making of a Legend

Stephen Howarth

Bene Factum Publishing

658·87

First published in 2003 by
Bene Factum Publishing Ltd
PO Box 33
Honiton
Devon EX14 9YD

www.benefactum.co.uk

ISBN 1 903071 06 2

Designed and Typeset by Spring O'Brien Ltd, London SW15 1AZ
Printed in Spain by Bookprint, S.L., Barcelona on behalf of Compass Press
Ltd, London

Acknowledgements

Henry Poole & Co and the author would especially like to thank Michael Wilkinson, military historian, for his exceptional work on the Company archives, and also:

Fiona Anderson, freelance curator and lecturer

David Bowcock, Cumbria Record Office

Sarah Davis, Archivist, Shropshire Record Office

Viscount Dupplin

Tracey Earl, Archivist, Coutts & Co

Friends of Highgate Cemetery

Reg Green, Official Historian, Aintree Racecourse

Guildhall Library, Corporation of London

Susan North, Costume and Dress Department, Victoria and Albert Museum

Oksana Sekatcheva, researcher and journalist

Francis Serjeant, Hammersmith and Fulham Archives and History Centre

Mrs Thomas J. Watson, Jr

Michael Wright, automotive artist

Contents

Introduction

One day late in April 1876, in the pleasant town of Brighton on England's south coast, a gentleman named Henry Poole decided to go out for a drive along the sea-front in his phaeton, a four-wheeled horse-drawn carriage.

He was sixty-one years old and was known, nationally and internationally, to be at the peak of his profession. But he was an ill man: he had had kidney troubles for the past two years, and recently had suffered a stroke. Taking 'carriage exercise' in the fresh air, especially sea air, was supposed to be good for the health, and his phaeton was the Victorian equivalent of a small stylish sports car today. Drawn by two horses, it contained two forward-facing seats and was built lightly for speed. It was also open-topped, without the option of a cover, and should have been ideal for an early spring afternoon.

Henry Poole had all the material trappings of Victorian commercial success. He owned the freehold of his business premises in London's Savile Row – a street which, over the previous thirty years, he had made world-famous. His horses were judged to be among the most beautiful in London. His leasehold Brighton house, 118 Marine Parade, was a grand, spacious family home overlooking the sea, and his freehold town house, Dorset Cottage at the end of Crabtree Lane in Fulham, was a large comfortable building with a big garden on the north bank of the Thames. He kept a steam launch there for jaunts on the river, one of his favourites being to follow the annual Oxford/Cambridge University Boat Race, taking a fine picnic lunch for his many illustrious friends.

Little of that is left. The Italianate premises in Savile Row have been replaced by a multi-storey building. Crabtree Lane still exists, but Dorset Cottage and its garden were long ago sold, demolished and built over. The steam launch has gone too, and 118 Marine Parade is part of a low-grade hotel.

By every appearance – not least his impeccable clothes – in 1876 Henry Poole was a wealthy man. Yet appearances can be deceptive: he was actually deeply in debt. He might not have known exactly how bad his debts were, but it seems likely he had a good idea of their extent, and that he was not only physically ill but experiencing mental distress as well. And when he took his supposedly health-giving drive that April day, the weather proved treacherous: in the words of one of his obituaries,

Henry Poole – the master tailor who took both his company and Savile Row to world prominence, photographed probably at the age of forty.

published just four weeks later, his phaeton was caught in 'our last severe snow storm'. He returned to 118 Marine Parade badly chilled. The chill developed into pneumonia, he suffered another stroke, and soon he knew he was close to death.

A relative named Edwin Cutler was among those who attended him in his last days, and Henry implored him to convey a dying man's last message. Cutler agreed, but was badly puzzled as to how he should do it. Henry died on 4 May 1876, and on 22 May Cutler wrote a letter to Henry's cousin and business associate Samuel Cundey:

> *My dear Cundey,*
>
> *I know how fully your time is occupied, but in consequence of a promise extracted from me by your poor Cousin, on his deathbed, I feel bound, in the most urgent manner, to impress in you, as soon as possible, to consider the best mode of faithfully carrying out his intention.*
>
> *On 3 separate occasions, during the last week of his life, more especially in the <u>very last time</u> he ever spoke to me, he made me faithfully promise that I would consult with you, as to the best means of conveying to His Royal Highness the Prince of Wales "the deep feeling of gratitude, & (if the expression may be used) the respectful affection, he entertained towards His Royal Highness for all the many kindnesses & condescensions he had experienced through so many years, & that in some form, he wishes to His Royal Highness,*
> *<u>Farewell.</u>"*

It was rather a theatrical message, but as Cutler went on to say, Henry's link with the prince – the future King Edward VII – was 'an all-absorbing sentiment'. For Samuel Cundey, coping with the immediate aftermath of Henry's death, it was a simple enough matter to send the message round to Marlborough House, the prince's residence. A reply came from a courtier:

> *I have shown the letter you left this morning to the Prince of Wales who desires me to assure you how touched he feels at the messages which were left for him by Mr Poole.*
>
> *His Royal Highness as you are aware had a great regard for him, and looked upon him more in the light of a friend than in any other point of view.*

This was a generous and a fairly remarkable thing to say, for Henry Poole had not been an aristocrat or even a member of the gentry: he was a tailor, a tradesman. Yet he was such a skilled tailor and extraordinary man that he could truthfully claim the friendship of many princes, kings and emperors.

However, as Henry's complex Will was unravelled, Samuel Cundey discovered that these noble friendships had come at a price. Skilled as Henry and his workers were at tailoring, engaging as he was as a companion, he had nonetheless been dreadful as a businessman, and when he died in 1876 after thirty years as 'king of the Row' his debts nearly crippled his business; and his relative Edwin Cutler soon introduced astonishing problems, creating a twenty-nine-year legal battle for ownership of his company.

Poole's dates its history from 1806. The fact that it survived Henry's death owes much to the efforts of Samuel Cundey and his cousin Mary Ann, Henry's sister; without them the firm would have vanished. Today Henry Poole & Co still flourishes, and is rightly regarded as the founding firm of Savile Row. It was not the first tailoring establishment to set up in the Row, so to give it this distinction may seem curious. But the two or three preceding firms were short-lived, and although some now operating there began earlier than Poole's, they did so elsewhere and only came to the Row because of Henry Poole's example. Henry became literally a legend in his own lifetime, and with his style and panache, by the time he died he had turned a London street-name into a worldwide synonym for the very best in gentlemen's bespoke tailoring.

This book tells his story and that of his family, because apart from being the founder of Savile Row, Henry Poole's (now approaching its seventh generation) is also the only firm in the Row to have remained resolutely family-owned and family-managed since its beginning. To return to its beginning, we must go back more than seventy years before Henry's death, to the era of the Napoleonic War – because improbable as it might seem, that war was the beginning of the tradition of supreme British tailoring. But first we should go back even further, to the origins of Savile Row itself.

CHAPTER 1

Before the Row became The Row

The phrase 'Savile Row' has at least three connected meanings. Firstly it means the actual Row, or Savile Street as it was called at the time of its construction. Secondly, 'Savile Row' has come to mean an outstandingly high standard of tailoring for ladies and gentlemen, and because of that, it has occasionally been called the champagne of tailoring. There is something in the comparison. The wine-makers of Champagne have long defended their right to the sole use of the word 'champagne'. People in other parts of the world may use the same methods to produce sparkling wines of similar quality, but the wines are not 'real' champagne. Likewise, tailors outside Savile Row may be able to make garments of similar quality, but unless they are located in the Row or its immediate vicinity, they are not making Savile Row garments. And that leads to the third meaning of Savile Row, because when it comes to supreme tailoring, Savile Row is not only a street but an area: Savile Row tailoring means tailoring from the Row and a recognized limited handful of tailors in other nearby London streets. Those nearby are Clifford Street, Conduit Street, Cork Street, Old Burlington Street and Sackville Street. Slightly further afield are Maddox Street, St George Street and Stafford Street, and further still are Dering Street, Mount Street and Princes Street, each being home to at least one of the fifty-four or so firms that can properly call themselves Savile Row tailors.

A 17th-century 'piccadill' after which Piccadilly was named. The piccadill supported the elaborate ruffs such as those worn by Queen Elizabeth I.

Fifty-four firms, twelve thoroughfares, eleven streets – and only one Row. The first known tailor to work close to that area was a Robert Baker, who in the very early 1600s was busy supplying fashionable folk with piccadills, extravagantly large embroidered ruffs worn around the neck by stylish Elizabethans. The ruffs were supported by silk or linen reinforced with card, whalebone or wire, and the term 'piccadill' had a double derivation from Spanish: each of the reinforcing shafts was like a little lance or *pica*, as used by the picador in a bullfight, and the ruffs were *pica-dilli*, the plural diminutive of *picado*, meaning 'pricked'. These elaborate pieces of neckwear were so popular that when Baker built himself a house it was nicknamed Pickadilly Hall, and when the area began to be developed, one of the nearest large roads was formally named

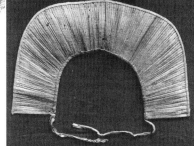

Piccadilly, as it still is. There cannot be many national capitals that have a main road called after a garment, but – as will be seen again in this book – tailors can sometimes have unexpected influence.

London's physical development was slow, and although Savile Row and its surrounding streets are only a few hundred yards from today's Piccadilly Circus, they remained essentially open meadows and fields for more than forty years after Baker's death in 1623. Further development was noticeable in the early 1660s as various noble houses were erected along Piccadilly, but the main impetus came when the City of London and its East End fell victim to the devastating plague of 1665 and the Great Fire of 1666. With those, there was a real motive for the wealthy to move westward, and London's West End began to take shape.

One of the early movers was the multi-titled Richard Boyle. He was knighted at the surprisingly early age of twelve, and in 1643, aged thirty-one, he inherited his father's title in the Irish aristocracy, becoming second Earl of Cork. In the same year he was granted an English title, Baron Clifford of

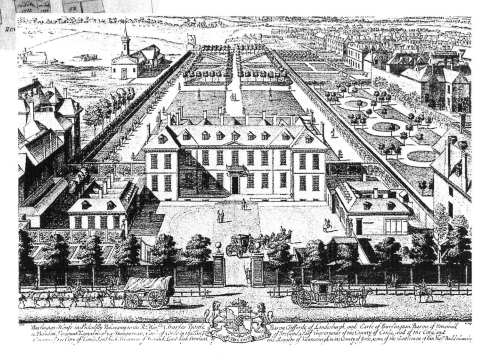

Burlington House in the 17th century (right). The gardens subsequently were developed and became part of the Pollen Estate, as the plan (above) of 1796 shows.

Lanesborough, and in 1663 he was created first Earl of Burlington. It is no accident that so many of the streets around Savile Row bear various of his family names, because after his Piccadilly mansion was completed in 1668, he went on to buy the lease of several acres of land to the rear, where those streets now stand.

Seeking some privacy, he surrounded his park with a brick wall, but this did not keep out the noises and smells of some adjacent businesses: a foundry, and a glassworks whose owner acquired one of his necessary chemicals, saltpetre, by the daily boiling of large quantities of 'night soil' – specifically urine. (The name Glasshouse Street commemorates that unsavoury neighbouring factory.) Despite Burlington's many attempts to have these works moved, they remained active until shortly before his death in 1697, and thereafter it fell to his grandson the third earl (also called Richard) to give the family's walled acres the form they largely hold today. The third earl has been described as 'a patron of literature and art, [who] spent large sums of money in gratifying a taste for architecture', which was certainly true. He had a huge annual income (£24,000 in money of the day, equivalent to perhaps £1.75 million in 2002) and cheerfully spent all of it – and more – firstly on remodelling Burlington House in the neo-Palladian style, and then, in order to supplement his income with their rents, in building Boyle Street, Clifford Street, Cork Street and what is now Old Burlington Street.

All this made a tremendous splash, and in the early 1730s he erected New Burlington Street and Savile Street, naming the last after his wife's family. The 'new pile of buildings' soon attracted good tenants, of whom the Countess of Suffolk was one: she lived at number 15 Savile Street (or Savile Row as it became) from 1735 until her death in 1767, and although the original building was replaced in 1887, since 1982 that address has been the home of Henry Poole & Company. Other tenants of similar social standing – generals, politicians, nobility, genteel widows – made the area an immediate fashionable success, but Lord Burlington continued to spend so freely that their combined rents were still not enough for him to make ends meet, and by the end of the decade he was obliged to sell his Irish estates in order to meet his debts of some £200,000 – in modern figures, £14.6 million or so. He died in 1753, not yet sixty years old.

He may have been an amateur and a spendthrift on an epic scale, but, much influenced by Italian street-planning styles, the third Earl Burlington and his architects had good eyes for building. The earl also took steps to preserve the tone of his development: the buildings were never intended to be shops, but private dwellings, and their original sixty-year leases contained

Henrietta, Countess of Suffolk, (above). From 1710 to 1734 she was the royal mistress of George Prince of Wales, later King George II (below), and occupant of 15 Savile Row, Henry Poole's present location, from 1735 to 1767.

7

restrictions on the appearance of their frontages. The restrictions kept shopkeepers away, because no ordinary tradesman could set up business without a good shop window to display his stock; but others – professionals who relied more on reputation, particularly physicians and tailors – could and did.

The Savile Row area has been a centre of style since its very beginning, and its resident physicians were among those who made it so. Although their names are not widely remembered today, Simon Burton and John Arbuthnot were just two of the first. Oxford-trained Dr Burton was one of the Row's earliest inhabitants, moving there in 1732 and remaining until his death in 1744. His friend and near neighbour in Cork Street, Dr Arbuthnot, was a Scot, well known not only as a physician (he was Queen Anne's doctor) but as a wit and satirist. In that role, in a series of pamphlets criticizing the Duke of Marlborough, he fixed the character John Bull as the stereotype of Englishmen, and he was part of the Countess of Suffolk's circle, well acquainted with Jonathan Swift, Alexander Pope, John Gay and most of the literary lions of the day.

But if a successful physician could be welcomed in the highest levels of society, tailoring in those days was hardly seen as a respectable profession, and one of the legends dear to Savile Row is that when tailors began to settle there, the doctors were so affronted that they moved en masse to Harley Street. Like many attractive legends this has been truncated in time (the tailors did not arrive all at once, nor did the doctors leave all at once), but the fact remains that once the tailors started to appear, the doctors started to go, and Harley Street eventually became the *locus operandi* of the most fashionable and expensive of them.

By the 1790s, following their best clients westwards from the City of London, there were tailors at work in about nine streets in and immediately around the Burlington estate, including Piccadilly, and by 1806 one short-lived firm had set up in Savile Row itself, in its northern half beyond Clifford Street. One of the early tailors in the area was himself a landowner: John Maddox, owner of part of the land bought by the first Earl Burlington. Around 1810 Maddox's family managed to buy back the plot, and, emulating the third earl's habit of giving family names to the streets, they called theirs Maddox Street – a street which soon had an indirect connection with Henry Poole's firm, and which for many decades was a definite part of 'Savile Row'.

During much of the 1700s, war between Britain and France had been a constant theme. It was far from over when the 1800s began, and on the national and international stage, 1806 was an intensely dramatic year. Throughout it, the thoughts and actions of many people in Britain and everyone in continental Europe were dominated by one man, Napoleon Bonaparte.

For British people, the year began with the funeral of their national hero, Admiral Lord Nelson, on 9 January. The sea war against France had effectively ended with the annihilating victory which he and his friend Admiral Collingwood had won off Cape Trafalgar on 21 October 1805, and though Britons bitterly lamented Nelson's death that day, they knew that the great threat which had hung over them for a decade – the threat of French invasion – had been removed. But in Europe the land war continued, with Napoleon supreme. In December 1805 he had defeated the combined forces of Russia and Austria at the battle of Austerlitz; in February 1806 his Treaty of Paris forced Britain to declare war on Prussia; in August he decreed and achieved the end of the ancient Holy Roman Empire; in October he crushed the Prussian army at the battle of Jena; and in December he promulgated the Berlin Decree, declaring Britain to be in a state of blockade.

Against this turbulent background, another much more humble man made a decision which though small in the scale of events was important to himself – and eventually, in an entirely peaceable way, of importance to another Napoleon Bonaparte and to many other rulers and private individuals around the world. The man was James Poole, and company tradition holds that in 1806, he and his wife made the 170-mile journey from the Shropshire village of Baschurch to London.

With a family firm such as Poole's, inevitably family history blends with the business, and perhaps inevitably the earliest days of both are hazy. Yet though we must rely to an extent on tradition, records show some of the very early details quite clearly. On 25 February 1742, James's grandfather Thomas Pool (without an 'e') was married in All Saints' Church, Baschurch, to a Sarah Jones. Between 1744 and 1753, they had four sons: Thomas junior, John (who died in infancy), Richard and George. Thomas the elder was buried on 29 September 1766. The wedding of his fourth son George is not recorded in Baschurch; presumably the bride (another Mary, four years older than George) came from another parish, where with bride's privilege they would have been married. However, they came back to live in Baschurch, and there in All Saints' Church their children were duly baptised: first their daughter Mary (a popular name in the family) on 14 April 1778, followed by John on 22 June 1779, and James on 6 December 1781. After this fecund and tiring period the family moved to the then neighbouring village of Prescott. Today the gap between the two places has been filled in by houses, but on 16 October 1788 their fourth and last recorded child George, 'of George and Mary Pool, Prescott', was baptised like all the other children in All Saints', Baschurch.

Mary the mother was buried at Baschurch on 25 June 1814, aged 65. Mary the

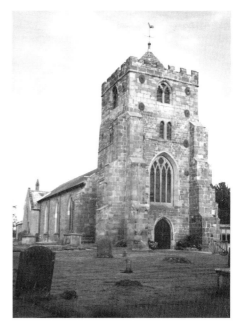

All Saints', Baschurch. *The local church to many generations of Pooles before James went to seek his fortune in London.*

daughter died the following year and was buried at Baschurch on 18 November 1815; she was only 38, and a spinster – she was listed with her maiden name, which was still spelt 'Pool'. However, by the time that George the father was buried just over two years later on 3 December 1817, the final 'e' had been added to the family name: he was recorded as 'George Poole'.

Meanwhile James had married. His wife, yet another Mary, was the same age as he, and came from the Shropshire village of Prees. Considering that Prees is fourteen miles by road from Baschurch (hardly the sort of distance one would travel on a whim in those days), it is intriguing to speculate how and where they met – perhaps at a market-day in Shrewsbury, the nearest town to them both.

Exactly why James became a tailor is a mystery, but his cousin Edward (Richard's son), nearly two years older, was a tailor, and to have two cousins in the same occupation suggests that it was already the family's trade. Moreover, in later years other more distant cousins who also lived locally were in the same or related trades: in 1835 'Poole and Wilkinson' were listed as linen and woollen drapers in the village of Wem, near Baschurch; in 1851 John Poole was a tailor in Prescott; and in 1859 Thomas and Samuel Poole were linen and woollen drapers in Shrewsbury.

In short, at an early date the family had the area sewn up, so to speak. James's cousin Edward (whose wife was 'keeper of the beer house' in Baschurch) stayed in the village all his life. But even today Baschurch and Wem are still small, and Shrewsbury is not a big town. James Poole sought a wider market, and with the help of his wife he found it. She had been married before, and as a widow she is said to have been quite well off: at least sufficiently so for the couple to uproot themselves from Shropshire and, in 1806, to undertake the long journey towards a new life in London.

James has been described in his Shropshire days as both a linen draper and a mantua-maker, a mantua being a kind of loose gown for ladies, sometimes made of silk. The record of his and Mary's first years in London is thin; the company archives contain only a reference to a lease assignment of 1806. But from 1812 it becomes definite, because certainly from then (and possibly from earlier) he set up shop as a draper – not yet a tailor as well – at 7 Everett Street, midway between Brunswick Square and Russell Square. The property was also their home.

All told, it was considerably different from Shropshire; yet while James and Mary Poole changed their lives with these decisions, Britain's foreign wars remained a distant but continuous background. In the summer of 1812 a new transatlantic struggle arose when the United States opened hostilities on the ocean. However, at the same time the land conflict with France was improving at last, as Arthur Wellesley (soon to be first Duke of Wellington) gradually drove French forces out of Spain and Portugal; and in the October, Napoleon experienced his first really major defeat. Facing Russia's insuperable defender, 'General Winter', he ordered the retreat of the remnants of the *Grande Armée* from the gates of burned-out Moscow. Starving in the snow, harassed by Cossacks and dying where they dropped, the horrors of the soldiers' withdrawal soon entered French and Russian legend alike.

During the weeks of that long retreat James Poole turned thirty-one years old, and it is worth emphasizing that apart from exceptional and short-lived periods of official but unreal peace, Britain and France had been at war throughout his entire life. Warfare then was not the 'total war' characteristic of the twentieth century, directly involving every member of the populace, but that does not mean it was much less frightening, or that people were less prepared to defend their lands when necessary. So, although there is no written record of what James Poole was doing between the winter of 1812 and the summer of 1815, we can assume he was getting on with his new London business and that he followed developments in foreign affairs with some relief and hope.

Like everyone else, he would have known that as Wellesley pushed through the Pyrenees from Spain to France, Napoleon's influence in Europe was becoming steadily reduced. He would have known too that in the spring of 1814, Napoleon abdicated as emperor of France and – no longer the arbiter of the continent – was exiled to the island of Elba, off Italy. But then on 1 March 1815 Napoleon returned to the mainland and advanced on Paris at the head of his reinvigorated army, and James Poole's more peaceable life became directly affected, because he joined a volunteer corps of infantry.

In national terms it seemed to be a critical time. In personal terms too there was good reason for him to take up volunteer arms. Fatherhood can change things dramatically and unexpectedly, and he was now a father three times over. His wife Mary already had a daughter from her first marriage, but the Pooles' first child together – a son named James – was born in 1809, followed by their daughter Mary Ann in 1812 and their second son Henry George on 8 November 1814. All were born at home in Everett Street.

James senior had spent his whole life in the shadow of war, and by joining the infantry, he probably wanted to do something to help shield his children from that shadow. If so, he succeeded, but not in the way he might have imagined. A copy of the birth certificate of his son Henry, held in the company archives, shows that by then James already called himself a 'taylor'. According to company tradition, the men of his volunteer corps were required to provide their own uniforms – not unusual at the time – and James and Mary together made his personal kit to such a high standard that others, including officers, asked for their own to be made by the same hands. This unplanned diversification succeeded so quickly and so well that by the time of Napoleon's final defeat at the battle of Waterloo on 18 June 1815, James Poole the modest linen draper was well on his way to becoming James Poole the prosperous military tailor, and his children were able to grow up not only in international peace – a condition completely unknown to their parents' generation – but as heirs to a strong family business.

James junior did not live to build on this: he died of consumption on 10 March 1843, aged only thirty-four. James senior died just three and a half years later, aged sixty-four. But Henry and Mary Ann survived. More than that, Henry inherited the business, gave it his own name, and expanded it enormously; and after his death in 1876, Mary Ann and their cousin Samuel Cundey ensured that it continued. Between them, the family created an English tradition that is still strong and vigorous: the tradition of Savile Row tailoring, led by Henry Poole and Company.

Poole's in the News

Exactly ten years after the Pooles moved to London, James unexpectedly found himself in the newspapers, bringing his name to a wide and no doubt captivated audience. He had been the victim of a burglary, and not once, but twice.

The first reported event took place on 15 December 1815, when baby Henry was only five weeks old. The affair came to trial a month later, and on 12 January 1816 *The Star* carried a brief account. It seemed simple enough: James had left his premises around 5.30 in the afternoon to visit a nearby customer. While he was out, two Bow Street officers saw a man go into the building and emerge with some cloth under his arm. James, returning, saw the man and two others walking down the street and 'immediately recognized his property'. Shouting 'Stop thief', he and the policemen gave chase while the three robbers 'instantly fled with precipitation', dropping the cloth as they ran. They were overtaken, apprehended and 'carried to Bow Street Office'.

The cloth was valued at five pounds. However, at the trial James acknowledged it was not quite dark when he left the premises, so the main question for the jury was whether this was 'a burglary in the night-time' or 'a stealing in the dwelling-house', in which case the value of the stolen property would for some reason be reduced to two pounds. The jury found the accused guilty of stealing in the dwelling-house, but from the prisoners' point of view, the distinction between the two types of crime was somewhat academic, because in either case a guilty verdict was 'equally penal in its consequences'. The most merciful sentence they could hope for was transportation to one of the convict colonies in Australia, but the likeliest was death by hanging.

So what might sound like a relatively petty offence was actually a serious business, and this trial was only the start of something much bigger. Nine months later, on 24 September 1816, a second trial took place, which *The Star* reported in detail next day. A well-thumbed copy of the original newspaper rests in Poole's archives;

Everett Street was the first location of Poole's in London, but the name no longer exists, having been incorporated into Marchmont Street.

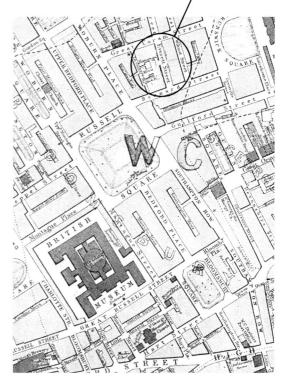

no doubt it was often read and re-read by James and Mary, and perhaps in later years by their children. Reading it today, it is remarkable how little people's interests and foibles have changed.

Health concerns figured prominently, with advertisements for medications such as 'Hickman's Pills' and the 'Cordial Balm of Gilead'. Alongside were other advertisements for lecture courses, new books, sales of property by auction, and the lottery. Further columns contained foreign news, editorial comment, shipping news, theatre reviews, announcements of marriages and deaths, bankruptcies, commodity markets ('the demand for Cotton continued extremely limited, and prices again gave way'), and crime reports. There were many of these, and among them all, the Poole episode stood out. *The Star* was only four pages long, yet it devoted more than three-quarters of one whole page to the trial, revealing much more than the first trial had done.

Readers could quickly see this was not a retrial or an appeal on behalf of the villains convicted in January. Two new defendants were in the dock, John 'Jack-a-Dandy' Donelly and George Vaughan. Donelly was an established police informer, and Vaughan was one of the officers responsible for the earlier arrests.

Bow Street Runners provided virtually the only law enforcement on the streets of London in the early 19th century. But as James Poole found out Runners themselves weren't always to be trusted.

Vaughan was given good character by three witnesses, but what emerged was a tale of corruption, deception, threats and incompetence – a 'most distressing conspiracy' which had required a 'long, painful, and anxious investigation'.

Two crimes had taken place, different but closely related. The first reported theft had occurred on the evening of 15 December, but James Poole had in fact been burgled for the first time the evening before, on 14 December. The operation had been set up by Donelly and Vaughan. Donelly had told the thieves of the temptingly valuable cloth and had led them to James's house, while Vaughan had lain in wait, ready to arrest them, with the plan that he and Donelly would share the court's expected reward money.

But the plot had started to unravel in a rather farcical way when Vaughan managed to miss the burglary. The next day he and Donelly agreed they should all have a second try. To be sure the building would be unlocked and the trap could be sprung, Vaughan went off to warn James Poole, taking another policeman with him.

So there was James, in the middle of December 1815, the victim of one burglary, and now with two Bow Street officers at his door warning him he was about to be burgled again. Vaughan introduced himself, gave James his card, and said: 'I know that your house is marked out to be robbed, and I am come, if you will let me, to take the men. I know they are very bad characters, and noted housebreakers; and if you don't let us take them, they will no doubt come when you are fast asleep, and most likely you, or some of your family, will be murdered.'

James quickly agreed to help. The policemen hid to watch events unfold. James, no doubt extremely worried, left the house on cue and saw the three burglars 'lurking about the street'. His wife Mary, who also knew what was happening, was still in the house. Presumably the children were with her too, and she had no protection apart from a servant boy whom James had told to hide on the stairs.

Vaughan's plan depended on everyone staying calm and doing exactly as he said, but as soon as one of the thieves came out, the second policeman gave chase prematurely. At the same time, James turned back, earlier than Vaughan intended, crying 'Stop thief!' Two thieves ran off in different directions, while the third dumped his loot behind the railings of Brunswick Square, bolted to Holborn, hailed a 'rattler' (a hackney cab) and made good his escape, picking up the cloth on the way.

But of course Vaughan knew perfectly well who they were and where they would be, and as we know, all three were duly arrested and put on trial. But then James unwittingly ruined Vaughan's plan, by saying it was not fully dark when the robbery began. The jury's decision (that this was not 'burglary in the night-time' but 'stealing from a dwelling-house') had no effect on the sentence, 'equally penal in its consequences'; but it did have an effect on the court's reward. A successful prosecution for burglary could bring forty pounds to the arresting officer; but even if successful, a prosecution for stealing from a dwelling-house brought nothing, and after the trial, an angry Vaughan said something which must have astonished James: 'You have leaned too much towards the prisoners by saying it was too light. You have deprived me of the three £40, part of which you would have had.'

This unguarded remark sparked off the 'long, painful, and anxious investigation' into the conspiracy between Vaughan and Donelly, who were eventually arrested and, in September 1816, 'capitally indicted' – placed on trial for their lives. The jury took only a quarter of an hour to reach their verdict: both were guilty.

The actual sentences for them and the three thieves are not clear. For any or all of them, the automatic sentence to death by hanging could have been commuted to transportation, possibly for life; but there is nothing to suggest that it was, and the Poole family tradition is that at least two were hanged.

However, it is an ill wind that blows no one any good, and as he read the newspaper reports of these frightening and stressful events, James may well have reflected that whatever the fate of the villains, in the end the adventure had done him no harm at all. Rather the contrary: his name, trade and address had featured in the articles on both trials, and thousands more people than he could ever otherwise have reached now knew the name of 'James Poole, a tailor of Everett Street.'

Bank Statement. *This 1819 ledger page of James Poole's account with Coutts Bank is Poole's earliest financial record. Coutts are still the company's bankers and in 1986 presented a copy of this page to the directors (see page 135).*

CHAPTER 3

Goodbye to Everett Street

London is like a living organism, constantly evolving, changing and reshaping itself. Rivers have been covered by roads and now flow underground: the river Fleet is one. Fleet Street, built above it in 1737, was for many years the home of London's newspaper industry, until rising costs and changing technology took the trade out to Docklands instead. There, at wharfs where tall ships once crowded in to load and discharge their cargoes, some of the city's tallest towers now stand. Names change too; for example, Everett Street, James Poole's first recorded London address, is now the southern end of Marchmont Street, and what was once farmland near Marylebone has become Regent's Park.

Driven by many forces, including the rise and decline of industries and simple changes in fashion, this evolution is a perpetual process in which every generation has a part; and in James Poole's generation, one of the most noteworthy changes was the transformation of most of the area lying between the Mall and Marylebone, commissioned by the Prince Regent and carried out by John Nash.

A map from 1827 shows how much had been accomplished by that date: the layout of the Park was already unmistakeable and many of London's most attractive streets had come into being, from Park Crescent southwards. Regent Street had already established a firm division between the elegance of Mayfair and the seediness of Soho, and had become a commercial triumph; and it was on 5 July 1822 that James Poole took a lease on number 171 Regent Street, on the street's west side.

The lease would run for ninety-nine years, with a fixed annual ground-rent of £90. In a short history of Poole's – a magazine article published in the 1950s – the shop was described as 'a big emporium', but it was not like a vast modern department store. A copy of the lease (a colossal document hand-written in copperplate on four sheets of vellum, each 27 inches by 22 inches) shows the building's ground plan: its frontage to Regent Street was just over 21 feet wide, with a depth of 52 feet going back from the street. At street level there was a big window next to the entrance lobby, which gave onto a corridor and stairs in one direction, and the shop in the other direction. The actual shop was essentially one very large room occupying almost the whole of that floor, with a smaller connected room at the back.

As with 7 Everett Street, 171 Regent Street was not only James's shop, store and workshop, but also the family home. Below ground there was a basement with three storage rooms, a washroom and toilet, while above the shop were three more floors with a total of seven rooms, a storage closet and another washroom and toilet.

Getting near to the Row. In 1822 James Poole moved his shop, and his home, to the elegantly fronted 171 Regent Street built by Nash.

Much of the street has been rebuilt since then, but the lease shows how firmly Nash stamped his influence on the original building. The leaseholder was obliged to maintain its appearance inside and out, and his duties were carefully detailed: indoors, repainting was to be done in August every fifth year, 'in good and proper oil colors', while every fourth year the outside wood and iron works were to be repainted 'in a good and workmanlike manner', with the window frames 'in imitation of Oak', other woodwork 'of stone color', and the iron railings and balconies 'the color of Bronze'. Most importantly, and probably most expensively, at the same time the leaseholder was also to 'recolor and rejoint in imitation of Bath stone the outside stucco'.

Taking on these costly commitments in London's most fashionable boulevard marked an important stage in James's career, indicating both his success and his ambition, and was no doubt done with the approval of his bankers, the elite Coutts & Company; their archives show that he had had an account with them since 15 July 1819. Coutts are still Henry Poole's bankers, but as one of the earliest surviving documents in Poole's own archives shows, James was soon experiencing one of the problems that can beset the tailoring trade or any other business where it is customary to give credit: bad debts. Dated 29 December 1823 and signed in his own hand, the document is a legal certificate. It does not give the full story (for

18

example, there is no mention of the amount due) but it records the name of the defaulter: William Blashier, described as a gentleman – someone who did not have to work for a living – formerly of Chancery Row, and more recently an inmate of the King's Bench Prison as 'an Insolvent Debtor'. Whether the money was ever recovered is unknown, but the certificate shows that James was at least prepared to chase debts if necessary. Unfortunately this was not a habit he passed on to his son Henry.

The certificate also shows that James was already in some form of partnership: it was made out in joint names, his and that of Alexander Geddes, a draper of 12 Great Ormond Street, an address within five minutes' walk of the old Everett Street premises. Geddes vanished from the story thereafter, and James's next, more formal, partnership did not last much longer. In 1826 he teamed up with a tailor named William Cooling, and the short-lived firm of Poole & Cooling was born. At first they traded from Regent Street, but on 31 May 1828 James took a lease on 4 Old Burlington Street (parallel to Regent Street, with Savile Row in between), and in the autumn of the year, subletting the Regent Street premises, he moved the joint business to Old Burlington Street.

Three other tailors had set up in that street in the preceding ten years, but it was almost as if James was gradually homing in on Savile Row; and although it is usually said that Henry Poole was the man who brought Poole's into the Row, in one sense Poole & Cooling were there already. The rear of Old Burlington Street gave onto the Row, where (as Post Office records show) they established a counting house and workshop. The firm thus had addresses in both streets, the one in the Row being at number 32 (later renumbered 38), and at least one contemporary directory lists James Poole, Tailor and Draper, as operating from 4 Old Burlington Street and 32 Savile Row from as early as 1835. However, in James's time the access at number 32 was only used as a staff entrance; his clients' entrance (no more than an ordinary front door, without show or display) was in Old Burlington Street.

And then even closer to Savile Row. In 1828 the business moved to 4 Old Burlington Street which, along with No 5, was demolished in 1961.

For reasons unknown the Poole & Cooling partnership was a failure: it was dissolved in 1829, and while James stayed put, Cooling moved to 47 Maddox Street, where he established his own business. Today, although his firm's name has changed to Wells of Mayfair and its address has changed, it still operates as a respected member of the Savile Row fraternity. Yet its start was somewhat murky, because when he moved, Cooling sent a letter to James's clients:

Allow me to return my most sincere and greatful acknowledgements for that kind preference so liberally given as to enable me during the period of my

19

management and cutting to encrease nearly double the Business of the late Firm. I now beg to solicit a continuance of the same encouragement to my new establishment trusting to my assiduity and unremitting attention to afford that entire satisfaction which I should hope that a long and active experience in Business will enable me to give. I have the honor to be, Sir, Your most obedt. and humble Servant.

Apart from its eccentricities of spelling, it was a fine example of the art of trying to poach clients in a discreet and gentlemanly manner. But the best part, which made it into a masterpiece, was kept for the end:

PS – As Mr Poole continues in the premises where the Business has hitherto been conducted, for the convenience of all parties, it is mutually agreed that he shall receive and pay all debts outstanding.

At this point James looked closer to home for assistance. James junior, by now aged twenty, worked for a stockbroker, so Henry was removed from school (the 'Academy for Noblemen's and Gentlemen's Sons') and taken into the business. He was not intended as a replacement for Cooling – he was still only fifteen – but his practical training began at once, and he followed the usual route for any tyro tailor, from sewing room to trimming room, then on from cutting room to fitting room.

He was entering a world which was not only specialized in its skills but increasingly so in its location. A few years later *The Town* newspaper noted how the parish of St. James's (which included the Burlington estate) had become home to more and more tailors, and that

Of all handicrafts, that of tailoring appears to be the most successful in modern arts – in the way of making (coining) money, we might compare it to witchcraft. The march of refinement has made rapid strides in this particular walk of scientific improvement. There is now no longer a tailor to be found in the classic region of St. James's. No! they are one and all professors of the art of cutting, "the development of the form divine."

The article described the area as 'this most delightful little village', still an apt phrase, and a remarkable number of tailors (according to the newspaper, sixteen separate enterprises) had congregated in eleven streets close to one another and their wealthy clients. Since then the shape of the village has changed; so have the names of most of the villagers. Clifford Street, Conduit Street, Cork Street and Old Burlington Street are still part of 'Savile Row', but St. James's Street, Poland Street, Ryder Street and South Audley Street – which all held leading tailors then – are distinctly beyond it. In those days Bond Street and Hanover Street had their tailors too, but the most striking difference is that when *The Town*'s article appeared in April 1838, Savile Row had none at all.

As for the 'villagers', the tailors themselves, just three of *The Town*'s commercial names survive in one form or another. Of course it is unusual for any company to last so long, but it is even more unusual for a company to last under the same name and ownership. One which has done so (but which, oddly, was not mentioned by *The Town*) is Davies & Son, in Hanover Street from 1804 until their move to Old Burlington Street in 1979. But of the three survivors from *The Town*'s listing, Meyer and Sons of Conduit Street (who were 'very old-fashioned, but very respectable … professors to majesty during three reigns') first transmuted to Meyer & Mortimer, then became part of Jones, Chalk and Dawson in Sackville Street. Similarly, Anderson of South Audley Street ('professors of high degree, and worthy of distinction') is now Anderson & Sheppard of 30 Savile Row. Poole's, already 'professors of the highest degree, [who] employ first-rate assistants', is thus unique: it is the only one of those sixteen firms to have kept both its name and its independence.

The comment about Meyer's being 'old-fashioned' introduces a new thread to this story of top-class tailoring: a brief history of the suit. If asked, many people would say that nothing could be more old-fashioned than this, Savile Row's staple product. On the other hand, most of those asked would have no idea about how suits evolved; but a little study of the history of male costume in England reveals many things. The three most important are these. Firstly, the three-piece suit originates from a combination of urban courtly life and English country sporting traditions. Secondly, for men this way of dressing is quite the opposite of the exclusive image of Savile Row: instead it is probably the most egalitarian male dress there has ever been. Thirdly, the Savile Row input is not one of fashion old or new, but of *style*.

A few words on these three, in reverse order. Style in clothing is like soul in music: if you have to ask what it is, you probably don't have it. Many tailors have tried to explain style in words; none has quite succeeded, but all have an instinct for what it is. 'Looks' come and go, style does not. Yet it is not immutable: it modifies with time and with each individual (or should do, although there was at least one Savile Row tailor – not from Poole's – who in the late 1980s claimed to have been making exactly the same design of suit for sixty years). In Savile Row terms, perhaps the most succinct and accurate description of style has been given by the trade paper *The Tailor and Cutter*: 'modernity with dignity'. The same publication took the actor Douglas Fairbanks Jr. to task when he remarked that 'the best-dressed man is the one who attracts least attention.' Not at all, said the paper: 'If good clothes were not noticeable it would mean they were in no way exceptional. A well-dressed man will always attract attention. It is merely that he does it unconsciously and naturally.' That may sound implausible, even pretentious, to anyone who has never been lucky enough to wear any tailor-made clothes; but anyone who has done will know that

The development of the modern suit and waistcoat (right, below and opposite) owes its origins to the simplified court dress and vest of Charles II through the adaptation of more elaborate dress of later generations.

King Charles the Second and Queene Catharine

there is practically nothing else which provides the same degree of comfort and quiet self-confidence, which radiates out as Savile Row style.

The egalitarianism of the outfit is more easily expressed. To cite *The Tailor and Cutter* again, for any man wishing to look smart without being too formal, the lounge suit 'is first favourite with prince and peasant, duke and dustman'. Democratic dress, in other words; yet before the suit evolved, democracy and relative equality were the last things any clothing would convey. Instead, clothes purposely expressed status, wealth or occupation, even if the dictates of fashion or rules often meant that they did so at the expense of comfort or convenience. It might fairly be said that a Savile Row suit is an expression of wealth or status; but compared to the ostentatious outfits of former ages, it is the soul of discretion, and the point remains that suits in general – two-piece or three-piece, Savile Row or not – are still amazingly egalitarian. The Savile Row suit is better than any other, but to choose Savile Row does not mean one is a better person, any more than the possession of wealth does; it merely means one is fortunate enough, and discerning enough, to be able to choose.

As for the suit's evolution, its first step took place in 1666 (coincidentally, the very time when the first Earl of Burlington was having his great mansion built on Piccadilly) and was an initiative of the English king, Charles II, in conscious reaction to the elaborate costumes of the French court under Louis XIV. This requires a little more historical background.

During Charles's eleven-year exile from Cromwell's England he had lived mainly in Holland and France, and at his restoration to the throne in 1660 he brought their fashions with him. However, it was

a time of acute economic competition with the Dutch, and in March 1665 a belligerent House of Commons man-oeuvred the unwilling king into a declaration of war against Holland. So began a disastrous two years for England. After some initial English victories, the Dutch more than held their own, then the plague came to London in 1665; early in 1666 Louis XIV declared war against England; and in the first four days of September the Great Fire raged through London.

Riding clothes (above left) further influenced the development of the traditional three piece suit (above) to the elegant clean cut lines of the 2002 executive suit (below) featured on the cover of The Robb Report.

Later events proved that Louis' real schemes were against Holland (in 1667 his forces invaded Flanders) but meanwhile, prompted by the expenses of the wars, King Charles made a symbolic – and as it turned out, a lastingly influential – decision. He announced to his court that henceforth he would wear a different, more modest and economical set of clothes, and on 15 October 1666 the diarist Samuel Pepys noted that 'this day the king begins to put on his vest'. The American War of Independence lay more than a hundred years in the future, but American English and tailoring English have both kept the word 'vest' to mean what it did in King Charles's day: not an undergarment protecting the chest from chills, but a half-way overgarment – in modern British English, a waistcoat.

Over the vest or waistcoat, the king wore what we would recognize as a coat or long jacket – 'a very fine and handsome garment', said one contemporary; 'a comely and manly habit', said another. Within two weeks most courtiers were similarly attired, and Pepys noted that the court was 'all full of vests [in] plain black'.

Once established by the king, the new mode remained, and as the *Encyclopaedia Britannica* said in 1911, 'The change, although the court was fickle, is of the first importance in the history of costume, for we have here the coat and waistcoat in a form from which our own coats and waistcoats derive without a break.'

The people who decided that this new model was a good idea, one

worth continuing, were the English country people: the rural nobility and gentry, down to squires and their associates – men whose main social pleasures were the equestrian pursuits of steeple-chasing, riding to hounds, and racing. The new courtly kit was adopted and adapted to fit with these activities, and in pictures and engravings over the following two hundred years or so, the evolution of the suit is clearly visible.

In modern fully formal men's wear – the morning suit and evening tail coat – the coat still closely replicates the hacking jacket of an 18th-century English gentleman. The cut-away front of evening dress was originally designed to clear the knees while riding; the tails, to fall each side of the horse; the two buttons in the small of the back, to hitch up the tails if the horse's flanks were muddy. Even the front buttoning, high on the chest, was placed there for comfort in the saddle.

It is curious to think that outfits which today are only worn on extremely formal occasions started as simple, practical sporting clothes. Nonetheless, that was the way of it, and when fifteen-year-old Henry Poole joined his father's workrooms he brought with him all that he had learned at the 'Academy for Noblemen's and Gentlemen's Sons', of which the most important things were, in the long run, a love of anything to do with horses, and a network of friendships in the sporting world; and it was from these – not only skill with cutting or sewing or trimming or fitting – that he began to make the name of Poole's into one of international renown.

CHAPTER 4

Royal Court and Racecourse

H enry Poole's training in his father's business made him into a completely competent practical tailor: having learned all the preceding levels of tailoring, he became the company's head fitter, the most senior man on the shop floor, and he would not have done so merely because he was 'the guv'nor's' son – it was too important a post. Anecdotes from later in his life, when he was famous, show that he knew his craft; one often-told story concerned 'a young puppy', an impudent fellow guest at a weekend house-party. In the billiard room after dinner, the young man:

> complained that his coat (made by Poole) did not fit properly. Without a word Poole took a piece of billiard-cue chalk, marked the coat all over with lines and crosses and then said, 'Take it to my shop when you get back to London and they will put it right.' The puppy must either have had the mortification of going up to change, or remaining a sight for the rest of the evening.

Of course it is unlikely that anyone present knew if the lines and crosses were accurate; another country-house tale about Henry has him as a guest of the Earl and

Rotten Row in the mid 19th century provided a wonderful showcase and point of social contact for young Henry Poole to show off the quality of his family's wares.

Countess of Stamford. After the visit he was asked who else had been there. 'Oh,' he said, 'a mixed lot, very mixed.' 'Come, come, Pooley,' was the reply. 'We can't all be tailors.'

There are several versions of both these stories, including one where 'We can't all be tailors' was said to him by the Prince of Wales. The tales may have grown in the telling, but the more important point is that they exist and were widely enjoyed, saying much about Henry's instinctive flair for memorable actions that helped to get him noticed and talked about.

He started to gain some public notice when he was still a very young man. At the age of twenty (undoubtedly courtesy of his father James) he was habitually driving a phaeton along London's other celebrated Row – Rotten Row in Hyde Park. Rotten Row's unusual name, a corruption of 'Route du Roi', originated under King William III, who had the road lined with three hundred oil lamps and made it the first artificially lit highway in Britain. Running from St. James's parish to the king's home at Kensington Palace, it rapidly became a fashionable rendezvous and is still the place where the capital's smartest riders congregate, a place to see and be seen.

Not that he was always in such congenial surroundings. His father would send him out on the road gathering orders and trying to collect payments, and a long letter home, dated only 'Sunday' but probably from this period, shows how much he hated this. He was in Newcastle in the north of England, and was 'heartily sick of this place as I am unlucky & can get neither orders nor money such as I expected.' Complaining about 'the fog (which seems constantly be here)', he added that with an improvement in the weather many customers had left town:

> On Friday evening I was walking about incessantly the whole of the time but could only get one order and no money. Indeed I think Scott went out of town to avoid me… I have no idle time as I have frequently to call 10 or a dozen times before I can get to see a party & then he tells me to call again, when I have the same trouble to meet with him as before.

In his exasperation he even had the nerve to take his father to task about the debts customers were allowed to run up:

> I have written and expect an answer from Robson who owes a heavy bill. I have also written to W. A. Surtees in the country whom I almost fear is a bad debt. B. S. Willsons and Dowsons [are] both decidedly so. Why give credit to such a man as Hunt of Cork Street, whom everybody knows to be such an unprincipled sharper & scamp, and also J C Ker? You will <u>never</u> get what you trust him for…

Frustrated and homesick, he continued:

> I am promised some orders from Snowball Thompson & Co & I shall then look

pretty close after the money... I am miserably tired of here. I shall be so very glad to get home again. I hope to leave here on Tuesday... I shall be so glad to get this journey done. I will however do all that is possible in money matters & nothing shall be left undone... Send me all the news you can when you write or if you cannot, ask Mother... Give my best love to her, and believe me, Your affectionate Son, H. G. Poole.

It was a most telling letter, revealing aspects of his character that would never change, especially the good financial intentions, the fatally conflicting dislike of business drudgery, and his deep-seated dislike of being out of the swim of fashion.

With his love of horses and the glamorous sporting world, Henry's simple desire was to associate with members of 'society', starting with the 'Noblemen's and Gentlemen's Sons' he had known at school. At first his father may have tried to discourage this, because there were clear risks: the young man could easily be tempted into spending beyond his means, or he could commit some awful faux pas, staining the reputation of the business. The question must have been discussed, but it is impossible to say for certain who dreamed up the creative solution. It could have been one of the parents, thinking back to the lucky chance that had moved James into his success as a military tailor; it could have been the youthful Henry. However, at some point it occurred to them that if he was seen out and about in all the best places, if he behaved himself well, and most importantly if he was wearing the best possible clothes, hand-made by Poole's, then he could attract new customers, probably wealthy and possibly influential.

Whether this was a calculated gamble or a sensible accommodation between father and son will never be known, but it was a good compromise, and it also offered a solution to another potential problem. A family business ought eventually to be either sold or passed on to the next generation, yet though James junior was the elder son, he had never enjoyed good health, and it seems that during his middle twenties, suffering from tuberculosis, he had to abandon work. Whether he would ever be able to participate actively in the business, let alone run it, could not be foretold. Mary Ann the daughter was next oldest and could inherit her share, but there is nothing to show she was trained in tailoring; James senior probably expected her to marry, perhaps within the tailoring profession, as his step-daughter had done. If so, he would have been disappointed, because Mary Ann never did marry; but anyway no one would have imagined her – a young woman – as the person to front an establishment that catered mainly for the military.

So within the immediate family, that left horse-loving Henry as the best, or the least unlikely, person eventually to succeed James senior. But the Poole clan was large, and in 1837 when Henry was twenty-three, James took another family member into the business: Samuel Cundey, his first cousin once removed. Samuel's parents were both first cousins to James, a fact recorded sixty years later by Samuel's

Keeping it in the family. Poole's benefited from the appointment of Henry's first cousin Samuel Cundey – a very wise action, as time proved.

own son Howard. The only other information known about them is that Samuel's father Joseph was a licensed victualler, 'a publican licensed to sell food and drink for consumption on the premises', usually with the emphasis on the drink rather than the food. There were other family links between publicans and tailors: back in Baschurch in Shropshire James had another cousin, Edward, whose wife was 'keeper of the beer house', and later on Samuel Cundey married the daughter of a publican.

When Samuel came into James's firm he was only fourteen, even younger than Henry had been, and like Henry he spent his entire working life there. He was taught tailoring too, eventually describing himself as a master tailor, but he was brought into the business as a clerk in the counting house. There he displayed sufficient aptitude for figures to become, in due course, the superintendent; and as his son Howard remembered in 1897, he also became Henry's 'other self to all customers', because after James senior died, the two cousins ran the company together for a full thirty years, and Samuel for a further seven years thereafter. Each of them made their mark on it, but in very different ways. Henry, senior both in age and in status as the son of the proprietor, built it into the world's leading firm of tailors; and in the nightmare period after his death Samuel rescued it from his reckless management and enabled it to continue.

But when James senior was still alive and Henry and Samuel were still young, the late 1830s must have been an exciting time for them all in their different ways – especially the year 1839, both for James and Henry. James enjoyed a signal success that year: he submitted a new design for formal dress at the royal Court, and the design was accepted. As for Henry, his best friend in the sporting set won the first official Grand National steeplechase at Aintree near Liverpool. These contrasting events were both important to the Poole family and their business, and each is worth a closer look.

The acceptance of James's Court Dress design was the pinnacle of his professional life, and it does not diminish the achievement to say that his design was only one among several that came into use under the new young monarch Queen Victoria, who had succeeded to the throne in 1837. The new designs replaced and sought to simplify those of the Georgian period, which (apart from anything else) were very heavy. Anyone attending a court function had to wear the appropriate formal outfit, and James's was for 'Gentlemen who do not wear Uniform'.

It came in two versions. The first consisted of a single-breasted tailcoat, waistcoat and breeches all made of black silk velvet, with the front of the coat 'cut small' (to be worn open and unbuttoned), along with black silk hose, black patent leather shoes, a cocked hat of black beaver or silk, a white bow necktie and white gloves.

Buttons and buckles were of cut steel, with the coat buttons being purely decorative. (There were six at the front, with dummy buttonholes, two at the back of the waist and two at the end of the tails or 'skirts', and the coat overall was a clear descendant of the rider's coat.) The coat had a 'stand' collar and plain 'gauntlet' cuffs; pockets to each side, with flaps; a breast pocket; and a further discreet pocket or two hidden inside the skirts. Its body was lined with white silk and its skirts with black, and as an alternative to black silk velvet, the waistcoat could be of white satin ('*not* White Corded silk or White Marcella'). In either case the waistcoat bore four small buttons, matching those of the coat. The velvet knee-breeches ended with another three buttons, as well as buckles; and lastly, under the waistcoat, came the sword-belt of black silk web with a black velvet frog, the fastening.

The sword-hilt was to be of steel, with a black scabbard and steel mountings. The design of the sword-blade was just about the only part to remain unspecified, but since (like most of the buttons) the sword was purely decorative and not to be drawn from the scabbard, that probably did not matter very much.

The outfit was all very smart and, in this version, very sombre too, but there was a more cheerful alternative in mulberry-coloured, claret or green cloth, with gold buttons and a certain amount of gold trimming. However, if you chose the colourful cloth version, a different set of rules applied. In this case the waistcoat was not allowed to be satin at all, as in the black velvet version; instead, it had to be white corded silk or white Marcella, and whereas the black velvet outfit was quite versatile (it could be worn 'at Courts, Levées and Evening State Parties'), the cloth version *with breeches* could only be worn at courts and evening state parties: for levées the breeches and shoes were out, and instead it was essential to wear trousers with gold lace down the seam, and plain military patent leather boots.

All very complicated, and from the wearer's point of view it has to be said that the need for such a precise outfit is something of a mixed blessing, especially if it is for a one-off occasion. There is the expense, the unfamiliarity, the worry – is it all correct? Should the sword hang so, or so? – and anyone who suffers from dandruff is unlikely to want to wear black. But against the drawbacks is the memorable surprise on first seeing oneself in the mirror, decked out so well; the growing self-confidence, knowing that in fact all is correct; and the physical comfort of clothes personally tailored to enhance one's natural appearance. The anatomist Dr John Marshall was one of many who went through this precise experience. In the latter

Court connections began in earnest when James Poole's designs for a new order of Court Dress were given the Royal approval.

29

nineteenth century he lived in Savile Row, directly opposite Poole's (thereby incidentally disproving the legend that the doctors and tailors could not co-exist), and when he had to attend a royal function he immediately bought a 'Court dress of great gorgeousness' from his neighbour. Having dressed in his bedroom he emerged for inspection, 'rather nervous and amused and yet rather gratified too', and his gratification was only slightly marred by the servants' reaction: they were 'vastly amused', said his daughter.

With the acceptance of this design, the former linen draper and mantua-maker from Shropshire had really arrived, if not as a member of 'society' then as a recognized supplier of some of its needs. Acceptance did not have the cachet of a Royal Warrant but did indicate royal approval, bringing a distinct commercial advantage. James did not have a monopoly of manufacture (any tailor was permitted to make the Court Dress, provided it was done accurately), but for a gentleman who wanted the new design it was obviously better to go to the man who had originated it: James Poole of Old Burlington Street. And those who went to him for their Court Dress would very likely go to him for their more ordinary clothes as well.

While James savoured his achievement, Henry was enjoying the vicarious pleasure of his friend's victory in the Grand National. Originally called the Grand Liverpool Steeplechase, the 4½-mile race was held on Tuesday 26 February 1839, with seventeen runners. Horse-racing was the great national passion, followed with far more intensity and excitement than soccer or cricket, which barely existed as national sports. Although soccer was five hundred years old, surprisingly it still had no official rules or structure: rules were not drawn up until 1863, and the Football Association was not founded until 1867. Organized cricket was less than a century old (its first rules were drawn up in 1744), and even its most ardent modern devotees would admit that it lacks the visceral thrill of a short swift race between quality horses with expert riders, a spectacle which has electrified audiences since Roman times at least. Above all was the thrill of the gambling, which had to be done at the racecourse on the day, breathing in the heady atmosphere of crowds and competition.

Whether Henry Poole was present at the inaugural Grand National is anyone's guess. Probably he was not: from London to Liverpool is over two hundred miles and the railways were in their infancy – although the audience was no doubt swelled by the ten-year-old line from Manchester to Liverpool. But he would very soon have been told about the race by his friend Jem Mason, the winner.

'Dandy' Jem Mason – winner of the first Grand National (then called The Grand Liverpool Steeplechase) and young Henry Poole's great friend. No doubt the nickname 'Dandy' was thanks to the tailoring skills of his friend's family company.

Jem, son of a Huntingdonshire horse dealer, was twenty-three. His mount was the aptly named 'Lottery', running with odds of five to one. The course emulated a real cross-country steeplechase, including among other hazards a large stretch of ploughed land, a stone wall five feet high and various water-jumps. At the first of these, Brook No. 1, the leading horse Conrad took the jump badly and threw its rider Captain Martin Becher into the water. With sixteen other horses drumming along in hot pursuit behind him, Becher prudently stayed in the brook and let them hurtle over his head; and such are the vagaries of history that while only specialists remember the name of the first winner, millions of people know the name of Becher's Brook.

With the captain and Conrad out of it, Jem and Lottery went on to win almost at a stroll – the race remains the slowest ever recorded at Aintree, lasting nearly fifteen minutes from start to finish; but a win is a win, and in Jem's words, Lottery was a horse which could 'jump from 'ell to 'ackney'. The distance between those two places has never been accurately measured, but Lottery's final jump that day was thirty-three feet, and having beaten the best that England and Ireland could offer, Jem was acknowledged as the best of all cross-country riders.

For the Pooles and their business, Jem's victory, fame, and friendship with Henry offered the all-important oxygen of publicity. Wherever he went Jem was kitted out in the best that Poole's could provide, and other young sporting men saw him and followed, buying their clothes from Poole's.

This did not necessarily mean that they actually visited Old Burlington Street; it was quite usual for a tailor to be invited to his client's country home, sometimes with a full entourage of staff, to measure and make. One such client was the Earl of Stamford, in whose billiard room Henry was later said to have wielded the chalk. Stamford was not quite accepted in higher society: the woman he had married and made his countess had formerly been a circus rider. But middling society was less critical, and the earl was successively master of two important hunts, the Albrighton and the Quorn, introducing Henry to the members. They found this young man had interesting qualifications: he was friendly with the master, he could ride well, and his father's firm made very good clothes. Through these evolving connections and others, especially the London horse-loving fraternity that gathered to view and bid at the auctions at Tattersall's Yard on Hyde Park Corner, Henry brought valuable new trade into his father's workshops.

For a company that had come to prominence as military tailors it was a timely development, because with the end of the French wars, Britain had entered upon what proved to be a prolonged period of relative peace. Poole's now began to cater for sportsmen as much as for soldiers, and soon Henry's cousin Samuel Cundey took a most important step in his young life: on 24 October 1841, in the local parish church of St. James, he married a girl named Eliza Howard.

Samuel and Eliza lived at 4 Dover Street, just a short walk from his place of employment at 4 Old Burlington Street. The Dover Street address was and still is a pub, in those days called the Coach and Horses, and was Eliza's parents' business and home: her mother Anna Howard continued to run it after her father died.

The newly-weds were extremely young: Samuel was eighteen years and two months old, and Eliza just sixteen years and one month. At those ages both required parental consent, so the match must have been approved; and there was no reason not to. Samuel had steady employment with his increasingly successful cousins the Pooles, father and son, and it was no shotgun wedding – Samuel and Eliza's first child was not born until ten years later. Thus the marriage probably grew from and contributed to the happiest and most prosperous period the extended Poole family had ever known; but in the midst of that period a double tragedy was slowly taking shape.

What had become of James junior? It has always been said that after ceasing work because of his illness he lived permanently with his parents at 4 Old Burlington Street. However, by 1841 this was not so. The London census for that year shows ten residents there, of whom five were listed by name: James Poole, tailor, his wife Mary, their daughter Mary Ann, their son Henry, and a twenty-year-old relative called Mary Drury, described as an 'independent'. The five unnamed residents were two women servants (hopefully not named Mary) and three men servants.

James junior was not listed among the residents, and today nobody knows where he was living then. Possibly he was in a sanatorium or hospital. At any rate, the record only shows that he was no longer at home; but although he was chronically ill, it is clear that he was not expected to die just yet. This is evident from his father's Will, written on 5 December 1842, in which James senior made careful provision for every member of the immediate family, right down to his step-granddaughters Adelaide and Fanny.

James senior was a sober, diligent, skilful and hard-working man with a healthy level of ambition, a realistic attitude towards life and death, and a strong sense of responsibility. He assumed he would predecease them all and he left unequivocal instructions as to how they should all be supported thereafter. In particular, Mary as his widow would receive the leasehold of 171 Regent Street and from its rents James junior would be paid £130 a year, 'clear of all deductions, to commence from the day of my decease… by quarterly, monthly or weekly payments'. In due course, after the deaths of Mary and James junior, Henry and Mary Ann would inherit number 171 in equal shares. Meanwhile, however, Henry was to receive the lease of 4 Old Burlington Street outright, 'and the fixtures therein and also the implements and utensils of trade and the goodwill of my Business there carried on'. The only major condition was that Mary as a widow and Mary Ann as a spinster should be allowed to live there rent-free. This would lapse on marriage.

In short, by the end of 1842 it was already fixed that Henry would be the next tailoring Poole, and James senior had arranged for the support of all family members who were not expected to support themselves – the women and his sickly elder son. Then barely three months later, on 14 March 1843, he made a purchase which, though suitable for a good family, he must have felt was shockingly premature. For the sum of £21 he bought in perpetuity the grant to grave number 698 in Highgate Cemetery West. The property (a small but valuable piece of real estate, figuring as the subject of legal argument in the company's subsequent history) measured nine feet by six feet six inches. No doubt he would have bought a family grave before long anyway; he was too sensible a man not to. But James junior had died on 10 March, and the fact that his father did not have a grave ready for him shows how sudden and unexpected his death was.

Preparing for all eventualities. James Poole's purchase of a family plot in Highgate Cemetery in March 1843 undoubtedly was prompted by the sad death of his son.

James junior was buried on 17 March 1843, and it is probably not exaggerating to say that the death broke his father's heart. Infant mortality in England was high, yet James senior had never before endured the loss of a child, and for any parent there is no loss at any time of life which compares with that experience; so it may be that the death of his first-born son, coupled perhaps with a sense of guilt at being unprepared, hastened his own death, which came only three and a half years later.

Before then, ever practical, James senior took at least one further step to integrate Henry more actively into the business: in 1843 he renamed the company James Poole and Son. And there was one last twist in the tale of his life, a twist at least as unexpected as James junior's death, but so ironic that for James senior it must have been a source of amused pride. On 15 August 1846 the firm gained a

new customer. Giving his address as the Brunswick Hotel, London, the customer was Napoleon Bonaparte – not the deceased emperor whose escape from Elba had propelled James into the art of military tailoring, but his nephew Prince Louis Napoleon, pretender to the throne of republican France, who now placed an order for a superfine black frock coat, double-breasted, with silk linings to the body, skirts and sleeves: cost, £6/16/6 – six pounds, sixteen shillings and sixpence, or about £400 in 2002. He was Poole's first royal customer, and James Poole's first and last: James died five weeks later, on 21 September 1846, aged sixty-four. He was buried in the same grave as his son and namesake, and the business he had built up over a lifetime passed to Henry, still only thirty-one years old.

Proud of his Court Dress, James senior had prepared for this day as best he could. Even so, Henry was better known in the hunting field than in the fitting room, so perhaps it was not the most promising of prospects for a tailor's firm; but James could never have imagined how quickly and how completely Henry would eclipse his achievements and come to dominate the world of bespoke tailoring.

Poole's first emperor. While still pretender to the French throne and exiled in London, Prince Charles Louis Napoleon Bonaparte, the future Emperor of the French, became one of James and Henry Poole's most prominent clients.

CHAPTER 5

Into The Row

It seems that in 1843 Henry Poole tried not to let his brother's death affect him too much. With his father renaming the business as James Poole and Son, he must have been obliged to become more closely involved in its management, but he maintained his friendships in the sporting world. In 1844 Jem Mason retired from racing to set up a business at the Bell Hotel in the Buckinghamshire village of Winslow, forty miles from London, supplying fresh horses for riders in the Queen's Buckhounds, and Henry went off to join him: one of his own obituary notices states that he lived 'for some time' at the Bell 'with Jem Mason, where he had a first-rate stud of horses.' The Bell, a Georgian building on an earlier Tudor frame, is still there and is still a pleasant welcoming hotel, but the existence of the stud has made no impression on its history, where it has been totally forgotten. For Henry, the stud can only have been a part-time occupation at best, even when his father was still alive.

Court Tailor by Appointment. Building on his father's achievement of designing Court Dress, Henry Poole received Queen Victoria's Royal Warrant in 1869.

When he inherited the family business in 1846, this had to change. He was still a young man, still single, but the deaths of his elder brother and his father catapulted him – whether he liked it or not – into the positions of head of the family and of the firm, responsible for the welfare of his mother (who lived another sixteen years), his sister Mary Ann and their cousin (now his employee) Samuel Cundey. By extension he was also responsible for the welfare of Samuel's young wife Eliza, as well as the livelihoods of all the firm's other employees and outworkers and their dependants; and, as if all that were not enough change in his way of life, he was also going to have to curtail or at least modify his active interest in the sporting world.

He approached these challenges, personal and professional, with such tremendous vigour that when he died thirty years later, *The Tailor and Cutter* described him as 'head of the most noted tailoring firm in the world, both on account of its extent and the aristocratic element in its connection. He was tailor by appointment to all the crowned heads in the world of any note …'

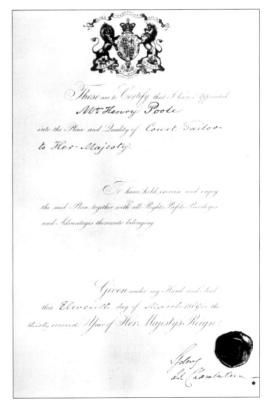

There was very little exaggeration in this extraordinary statement. A 'General Estimates' price-list from about the time of Henry's death was positively laden with imperial and regal crests of special appointment: twenty-two all told, headed by the most illustrious in the world at the time, the crest of Queen Victoria herself. Building on his father's highest achievement, the 1839 design of Court Dress, Henry became Victoria's 'Court Tailor by Special Appointment' in 1869.

The armorial bearings of her sons the Prince of Wales and the Duke of Edinburgh were also prominently displayed on the 'General Estimates' form. Those titles and a few of the others on his list still exist (the Prince of Orange and the monarchs of Belgium, Denmark, Spain and Sweden), but most of the distinguished names have vanished into history, emblems of another age. The Emperor of Russia, the Emperor of the French, the Emperor of Germany, the Kings of Greece and Portugal and Italy, the Shah of Persia and the Khedive of Egypt, the Crown Princes of Austria and of Prussia, the Grand Duke of Hesse and the Duke of Teck – all were customers of Henry Poole's, but all their titles have either gone completely or have lost their former prominence; and few people nowadays have even heard of Henry's other imperial client, the Emperor of Brazil. (There were in fact two such emperors, father and son, both called Pedro. Emperor Pedro II, who granted Henry his Warrant in 1874, reigned peacefully from 1840 to 1889, and was a remarkably liberal man, 'distinguished by his love of learning and scholarly tastes'. He promoted Brazil's national economic expansion, abolished slavery, introduced universal suffrage and secularized the civil service; but he was

Crowned heads flock to Poole's. Including Tsar Alexander II (top right) and his brother Grand Duke Constantine (opposite).

overthrown by the army and lived the last two years of his life as an exile, dying in Paris.)

Nevertheless, even if to us these people are emblems of another age, to Henry and his contemporaries they were the sublime emblems of their own age, respected, courted, admired and almost revered. To gain their custom and public approbation was a magnificent success – more than that, a magnificent series of successes – and to be permitted to display their names on his papers was a no less magnificent advertisement.

In 1846 Prince Louis Napoleon Bonaparte, the first of this illustrious parade to submit to Poole's tape-measure, escaped from five years' incarceration in the French fortress of Ham, where he had been condemned to 'perpetual imprisonment' for having made two abortive attempts to retake the throne of France. He made his way to England and there found a number of supporters, including Henry and one of Henry's other early distinguished clients, the banker Baron Meyer de Rothschild.

This was not just moral support but practical financial aid. The Rothschilds were already wealthy, and it is another irony that their family fortune was partly based on their superior international intelligence system in 1815, at the time of the battle of Waterloo and the final defeat of Prince Napoleon's uncle, the first Emperor Napoleon. But neither the baron nor Henry were supporters of republicanism, and they and others came together to help the prince with funds, allegedly to the tune of £10,000. This was such a large amount (in 2002, roughly equivalent to £600,000) that Henry can hardly have provided the prince with a significant proportion in cash. Indeed, the cash-flow may well have been more the other way around, because having begun purchasing from Poole's as soon as he arrived in England, the prince became a very good customer, with his orders showing the kind of garments preferred by any contemporary gentleman of rank.

For the last few months of 1846 these included pea coats (a kind of overcoat), trousers, waistcoats, and a shooting jacket – straightforward enough items, but made of beautiful materials. One of the waistcoats, for example, was of a fine grey figured double-breasted cashmere; another was of a rich grey stripe figured silk, and a third was of a rich stripe satin, all with silk back linings. Similarly, the trousers were of fine fancy check doeskin cassimere (a wool comparable to but not as grand as cashmere), while the shooting jacket was of green Angola (a blend of wool and cotton designed to imitate mohair or angora) with extra pockets and flaps and silk-lined sleeves. The pea coats were no less attractive and comfortable: one was of Venetian ('a fabric of an upright warp twill character, produced by a sateen warp weave with a dot added… a dress face woollen cloth') lined throughout with silk, with velvet collar, facings and cuffs, and the second (ordered early in November to meet the winter weather) was of blue waterproof Witney wool, bound with braid and lined with check Gambroon (a heavy linen), with a velvet collar and silk sleeve linings.

With those and a few other smaller orders, the prince's account for September-December 1846 came to just over forty pounds (about £2,500 in 2002 figures), which he settled promptly and – like the majority of contemporary clients – mostly in cash.

So there was Henry in 1846 at age thirty-one, London born and bred, undoubtedly believing himself more urbane and sophisticated than his country-born father James, and able to boast that a prince was his customer. But one customer, even a prince, is not enough for any firm, and Poole's naturally depended mainly upon its more ordinary clients, of whom there were at least several dozen (generally far more) at any one time. Before plunging into the swirling tide of royal and aristocratic clients which characterized Henry's most glittering years, we should sketch some of these, for they were the backbone of the business.

The evolution of evening wear from the tail coat to the version without tails, probably pioneered by Viscount Dupplin.

Once 'in the Poole', it was not unusual for customers to remain faithful to the firm for decades; one such was a Mr P.C. Wilkinson of Newall Hall, Otley, Suffolk, who placed his opening order on 7 May 1846, when James senior was still alive, and remained a customer for forty-three years. Over that period, firstly under Henry's management, next under Samuel Cundey's and lastly under that of Samuel's son Howard, Mr Wilkinson was re-measured several times as his physique changed with age, until at last on 27 July 1889 his account was ended with the single word 'Dead' scrawled across it. (This pragmatic form of closure was inevitably repeated many times over the years. There was one notable exception: on 17 February 1905 the account of Grand Duke Serge of Russia was terminated with the word 'Assassinated'.)

Introduction of new clients by satisfied ones was always a welcome means of gaining new business. Prince Napoleon introduced his brother Prince Jerome, and any family's name could crop up repeatedly; a few from Henry's first year in charge were the Joblings, Fifes, Siltzers and Marriotts. Mr T.W. Jobling of Jarrow, near Gateshead, introduced Mr M.L. Jobling of Percy Street, Newcastle, and Mr John Jobling of Seaton Lodge, while Mr J.B. Fife of Hood Street, Newcastle, introduced Mr Henry Fife of Westgate Square, Newcastle. Similarly, Mr John Siltzer of Manchester brought along Mr D. Siltzer, and a Captain Marriott (an army officer) brought his brothers Cornelius and Henry. Henry Marriott's first order, placed on 10 July 1847, included amongst other things a blue Witney yachting jacket lined with check Angola, with a silk velvet collar and silk sleeve linings – and a Patent Life Preserver, priced at seven guineas (seven pounds and seven shillings).

Introductions by friends were no less effective than family. Captain Marriott had been introduced by John Waite, the former owner of 4 Old Burlington Street, and at least once, Henry's old friend Jem Mason started a chain lasting decades and shading into the nobility theme. On 17 March 1847, Jem introduced the Earl of Strathmore to Henry. On 5 November that year, Strathmore introduced Viscount Dupplin; on 12 April 1848 Dupplin introduced an army friend, a Captain Farrer, followed on 30 May by a fellow nobleman, the Earl of Chesterfield, and on 9 December by Earl Mountcharles, who promptly ordered fifty-one pounds' worth of clothing, including a pair of blue beaver yachting trousers. Lord Dupplin, who in due course succeeded to his father's title and became Earl of Kinnoul, was himself a very steady customer, buying regularly not only for himself but also for his footman, groom and coachman; and he had the added inestimable virtue of paying his bills punctually, in full and in cash (even though it was only once a year) until 1 February 1897, when it became his account's turn to be endorsed 'Dead'.

As time went by, increasingly elaborate ceremonial outfits figured more and more frequently in the order books, but in these early days of Henry's reign the dominant orders were the standard items of any gentleman's wardrobe: waistcoats (more often double-breasted than single-breasted), trousers and frock coats. Nowadays reserved for formal occasions, frock coats were the staple coat for day-wear in town, indoors or outdoors, covered by

One of the most elegant men of his generation. Lord Dupplin was a great friend of the Prince of Wales and major Poole customer. The introduction of the dinner jacket is attributed to him.

a cape or overcoat if outdoors in bad weather, and were characterized by their length (the same back and front, reaching just below the knee) and their carefully shaped waist.

It is often thought that all these Victorian gentlemen dressed exactly the same and always in black, and because of Henry Poole's great influence on male fashions in the Victorian era it has sometimes been said that this was his fault. Yet although there was conformity, there was not total uniformity; frock coats might be double-breasted or single-breasted, with the front designed to button either to the top of the chest, to the breastbone or even just below, and no diktat said they must all be black: in 1848, for example, a gentleman called R. H. Hughes, Esquire, ordered one in superfine rifle green, double-breasted with silk linings.

Mr Hughes also favoured very relaxed and comfortable garments: his first order for 1848 was a superfine blue Venetian lounging jacket (a short informal jacket for

The frock coat was customary wear for all Victorian gentlemen.

indoor wear) and he loved his dressing gowns: one, which cost him five guineas, was of fine blue and red flannel with 'handsome cord and tassels'; another, at the same price, was in fine blue tweed lined with silk – an over-warm garment by modern standards, but very cosy in the nights before central heating. His bill for the year was a thumping seventy-nine pounds, reduced (by the standard 7.5% discount for cash, and by the very unusual return of a pair of two-guinea trousers) to a more manageable seventy-one pounds eleven shillings.

To put into some perspective the amounts these upper and upper-middle class gentlemen would spend on their clothes, it is worth noting that in 1886 (the earliest year for which figures are available), the average weekly wage for a British male manual worker was still only one pound four shillings and sevenpence. At that rate an average male worker would have to give up a full month's wage for just one of Mr Hughes' 1848 dressing gowns, and even when reduced to its final figure, his total clothing bill represented fifty-eight weeks' pay for a working-class man.

As yet there were no Warrants either royal or imperial to attach to the company paperwork, but Mr Hughes' account for 1848 shows several other aspects of the firm's business, first and foremost its new name and address. Instead of James Poole & Son of Old Burlington Street, it was now Henry Poole & Company, Tailors, of 32 Savile Row and 4 Old Burlington Street. This was the year when Henry renamed the company after himself. At the same time, exploiting his building's double-sided nature, he enlarged the premises, replacing the stables on the Savile Row side with a showroom, and there changed the former staff entrance into the primary public entrance. The authentic Henry Poole of Savile Row was born.

Next on Mr Hughes' account form came an outline of the firm's products: 'Ladies' Habits, Naval & Military Uniforms, Court Costumes.' We know about the military uniforms and court costumes; the former had been James Poole's passport to prosperity and reputation, and the latter his crowning accomplishment. Naval uniforms may have seemed a logical extension to military ones, yet Poole's found only limited success in that field. The firm's first naval customer was a Lieutenant G. A. Phayre, who placed an order in May 1846 – just within James's lifetime – but three years went by before its next, from Lieutenant (later Captain) W. Eyton. Moreover, although Phayre bought plenty of stylish civilian clothes he bought no uniform, and while Eyton did buy a blue undress uniform coat and a set of buttons, it was his only purchase for another three years.

Lieutenant Phayre must have been quite a dandy when off duty: his order included a black morning coat, a fancy figured cashmere waistcoat, ditto striped and quilted, three fine white quilt waistcoats, the making and trimming of a Persian Silk shawl waistcoat, one pair fancy blue stripe doeskin cassimere trousers, ditto in fine fancy drab, ditto in black cassimere dress, and a superfine brown pea coat of Circassian (a thin worsted fabric) faced with silk. He must also have been quite well off for a junior naval officer, because that little collection, ordered in one day, set him back twenty-four pounds – which may be why he did not return.

Eyton was a more modest spender: his uniform coat and buttons cost him five guineas in 1849, and his next purchase was scarcely extravagant, simply a cashmere waistcoat and some Angola trousers for three pounds thirteen shillings and sixpence in 1852. Perhaps he was away a lot, or perhaps he and Phayre had found out one of the great truths of Henry Poole's Savile Row: that however desirable it might be, quality of that standard does not come cheaply.

For a naval officer to be able to buy at Poole's, it helped to be senior and well connected. One of the firm's rare regular naval clients in the nineteenth century was Captain F. Beauchamp Seymour, later Admiral Lord Alcester GCB, who placed his own first order on 18 March 1852 and continued to buy both for himself and (from 1871) for Lady Alcester until his death in 1896. However, the main reasons for the paucity of naval personnel in Poole's books were simply geography and the fact that Poole's came late to the game. The fleet was largely based at Portsmouth, where naval outfitting had been the special province of Gieve's since 1785, when that firm's founder opened his first shop. During the Crimean War of 1854–56, Gieve's had a small ship actually in Crimean waters, providing British naval officers with their kit. After the war the company concentrated its efforts on the Royal Navy, and it became impractical for most other tailors to compete with the necessary special-ist skills or to contend with the handicap of distance. Poole's bowed quietly out of the naval market and did not re-enter it until 1905.

The other line introduced by Henry and listed at the head of Mr Hughes' account form was ladies' riding habits, allegedly made to cling so close that in the fitting stage they had to be sewn 'over the client's bare skin'. Hitherto it has been thought this glamorous innovation did not occur until 1857, but in fact the first young woman to receive a riding habit from Poole's was a Miss E. Waite (possibly the daughter of John Waite) who was measured on 27 July 1847. She was followed in July 1848 by Lady Jane Moore and Lady Helena Moore, daughters of the Earl of Mountcashell, who had started buying from Poole's the previous month. The daughters were each supplied with a silk-lined habit in superfine rifle green cloth at a price of ten guineas each – but price, in the earl's view, did not equate with cost.

For Poole's to supply riding habits emphasized the company's shift in focus from the military to the sporting field, but in these very orders we can see retrospectively the seeds of the disaster that Henry was sowing. In just four weeks in June and July 1848 Lord Mountcashell ran up a bill of seventy-five pounds and three shillings. Had he echoed his name and paid in cash he could have enjoyed the standard 7.5% discount. He did not, so after twelve months the account became subject to the usual 5% interest. And again after another twelve months – and again – and again…

In July 1863, *fifteen years* after the riding habits had been made and long after they must have been completely outgrown, if not worn out, the account was still unpaid and forty-three pounds of interest had accrued, increasing the debt from seventy-five to a hundred and eighteen pounds; and another eight years later in 1871, it still remained unpaid.

To imagine that it might ever be paid was to live in a dream world. In 1822, when James Poole had to take legal action against a debtor, he left no record of the amount involved, but it was probably only a few guineas. Mountcashell's original bill would have paid the ground rent on 171 Regent Street for nigh on ten months. In his worst nightmare James could never have dreamed that half a century later, his son would allow such an amount to stand on the books, possibly even counting it as one of the company's assets. It was sheer economic lunacy.

Yet Henry was not quite so culpably negligent as this suggests, nor did he acquire his customers because they thought he might supply them for nothing. Most, whether noble or not, paid promptly. Prince Napoleon did; so did the Earl of Lisburne; so did Mr Jasper Gripper. Lisburne (another aristocrat who came on board in James's last months of life) swiftly ordered over twenty-three pounds' worth of clothing, and paid in full when asked. Mr Gripper was as unusual as his name, placing orders which were frequent but always in small amounts (none more than sixteen pounds, with an average of about ten pounds), and he too paid in full when asked.

The fault lay almost as much in the system as in Henry. The system ran on credit, in a double sense: firstly the financial credit allowed to the customer by the supplier, whether he was a tailor, boot-maker, hatter or wine merchant; and secondly the social credit reflected on the chosen supplier by the customers. The desirable social credit attracted further customers, all expecting financial credit, and an expanding circle was formed. However, whether it became a commercially virtuous circle or a vicious one was something which depended on the priority the supplier gave to that bald and vulgar commodity, money.

If customers were unresponsive to their bills, then enticing their actual payment could be a delicate task. This was a problem faced by every tailoring firm, but one to which Henry was averse; no craftsman wished to wheedle, and he did not have the tactful dexterity of one of Gieve's managers – 'Surely, my Lord, you do not expect Mr Gieve to accept an order for yet another uniform before you have paid for the greatcoat which you have been wearing these past two winters!'

As increasing numbers of ever more distinguished clients came onto the books at 32 Savile Row, Henry became progressively less the great craftsman (which he had been), progressively less a sensible businessman (which he may have been), and progressively more the gentleman that he wished to be. But to combine the three qualities is rare, and is probably more difficult for someone starting as a craftsman and businessman and aspiring to be a gentleman, rather than vice versa.

Henry Poole failed to make the triple combination because he chose to pursue appearance over substance. In making this choice he had role models enough amongst his clientele – aristocrats who were rich in titles, even rich in property, but short of cash. From his clientele he had other potential models as well, clients rich in titles, property and cash too, such as the Rothschilds, who flocked to him in the 1850s. Solomon de Rothschild began ordering from him in 1851, as did Baron Nathan of the family's Paris branch, while Baron Charles and Baron James became his customers in 1852, Baron Meyer in 1853, Baron Alphonse in 1857 and Baroness James in 1859. But theirs was a model he could not follow all at once, and he chose not to follow the more modest model of a client like Jasper Gripper, buying often but in small amounts and always paying his way. Instead he chose to pursue the appearance of wealth, and if he had been challenged he could probably have made a plausible business case for it. Presenting the show of prosperity enhanced his firm's attractiveness to clients old and new;

Lionel de Rothschild. Following the regular flow of royalty and landed aristocrats, new more commercial – and increasingly influential – customers, as exemplified by many of the Rothschilds, now came to Poole's.

therefore the greater the show, the greater the implied prosperity, the greater the attraction, and the greater the future real prosperity.

In this he was not altogether wrong. Show can be important in business, and when his father James had let him drive around London in a phaeton, the same principle had applied. But no business can think of surviving solely upon show: to succeed and endure, there must be good consistent products and cash-flow at the root. In James's day there had been, and now, in the developing concept of Henry Poole's Savile Row tailoring, there were still the very highest quality clothes – which was why people of such different rank as Prince Napoleon and Mr Jasper Gripper bought their clothes there, and continue to do so. But Henry allowed too many people to acquire their clothes rather than buy them.

The difference between James and Henry was simple and crucial. James provided top-class tailoring, as did Henry; but whereas James had caution and modesty, building step by step on a solid financial base, Henry did not. Ignoring his own advice to his father in that letter from foggy Newcastle, he gave credit even when he had little or no prospect of it being redeemed, and in the pursuit of show he took on massive debt. As we shall see in later chapters, after decades of fine appearance, this was the ruinous combination he left to his inheritors.

Nevertheless, we today should give credit where credit is due: credit to his professional tailoring skill, to his often noted personal charm and pleasant character, to his courage, ambition, style, self-confidence and panache – to all the qualities from which he created the Savile Row tradition. It was only in the longer-term financial aspects of his management that he failed to deserve credit, and only those who suffered thereby were entitled to criticize him; and they kept their criticisms private. They were family, after all.

The Life of a Gentleman

Henry's first major property acquisition came when he decided to abandon the tradesmanlike habit of living above the shop. Instead, in the summer of 1851 he bought the freehold of the Crabtree Estate, a small riverside domain in semi-rural Fulham, just over four miles from Savile Row. 'Estate' was rather a grand term for the three-acre tract, but it was the official term, and may have appealed to him with its echoes of a gentleman's country residence. The land had three hundred feet of river frontage, and Dorset Cottage, the house at its focus, became the family home. He began to fill it with a growing collection of water-colours, old violins and French furniture, and over the years it also became the venue for popular parties, with his favourite and most valued clients as guests. In that respect no doubt he felt it was a thoroughly worthwhile investment; yet it proved much less so when placed in the actual balance sheet. In 1872, after twenty-one years of residence, a valuation was done of all his freehold and leasehold property, and he estimated that with purchase and improvements the Fulham house and acreage had cost him £16,000 – a million or so in 2002 figures; but the same valuation assessed its worth as no more than £10,000.

Dorset Cottage was not his only showy purchase in 1851. That was also the year of the Great Exhibition, brain-child of Queen Victoria's husband

Moving up and away. In 1851 Henry Poole's increased wealth and position in society was manifested by his purchase of Dorset Cottage (left) on the Crabtree Estate in Fulham. The local pub – The Old Crabtree (below)

Prince Albert. Housed in the gigantic Crystal Palace, an innovative glass and iron building erected for the purpose in Hyde Park, it had an intoxicating impact on the nation: England's population at the time was eighteen million, and by the time the exhibition closed after five and a half months, six million had passed through its gates. Henry Poole was one of its admirers, and when it was over he bought as many as possible of its accoutrements – statues, vases and bronze-framed mirrors – to enhance his showroom, which he further embellished with fourteen columns of Cornish marble, and enlarged with the addition of a gallery later known as the Peers' Gallery: he used it for the storage and display of many of the ceremonial robes commissioned from his shop.

After a mere five years as head of the firm, his order book was already starting to read like a directory of the peerage, British and foreign. Taking the list only to 1851 and only to the letter H, it included Viscount Barrington, Baron Bethmann Hollweg, Earl Beauchamp, Prince Napoleon Bonaparte, Prince Jerome Bonaparte, Count de Boutourlin, Earl Cairns, the Earl of Cork, Viscount Cranbourne, Lord Crencorne, the Earl of Chesterfield, Lord de Clifford, Marquis Conyngham, Lord Dacre, Lord Deramore, Lord Dorchester, Lord de L'Isle and Dudley, Lord Dunkellin, the Earl of Durham, Lord Gardagh, Marquis Garofalo, Baron de Godin, Lord Gough, the Earl of Harrowby, Lord Hopetown and Earl Howe – and there were at least as many peers, if not more, in the balance of the order book's alphabet.

The accelerating acquisition of aristocratic clients is the single most striking feature of Henry's regime; it is astonishing to see how many he gained, and how quickly. There were two reasons for this: firstly the very high quality of the product, Poole's clothing, combined with the effectiveness of Henry's marketing by example; and secondly the comparatively small national population and the stratification of society, which enabled a family firm to start a snowball of success and achieve great influence. In modern parlance, Henry instinctively knew his target market and how to exploit it fully.

Not just a gentleman's tailor. Eugénie de Montijo, fiancée of Prince Louis Napoleon and later Empress of the French, was just one of a number of female clients.

Ladies also featured in his client list: Lady Jane Churchill, Lady Hopetown, and in 1852 the most prestigious of all, the Spanish Countess Eugénie de Montijo, fiancée of Prince Napoleon. Elected president of France in 1848, the prince began to make his controversial mark on European history in December 1851 with a coup d'état, cancelling the constitution. After a successful plebiscite a year later he assumed the imperial title, and in January 1853 he married Eugénie. France was once again ruled by an Emperor Napoleon, and Henry had not only an emperor but an empress among his customers.

To celebrate, he took a trip to France late in the year, staying at an appropriately smart address – the Hotel Windsor on the Rue de Rivoli in Paris, where he received a chatty letter from his cousin Samuel Cundey, managing the company in London. Business was going well and had received a boost from the contemporary custom of 'mourning suits' – outfits made to order on the death of a distinguished individual. On Friday 25 November a gentleman named Sir John Guest had died, and on the following Monday, besides doing 'pretty well of trade in the ordinary way', Samuel had received orders for twenty-five 'Suits of Mourning for Sir John Guest's sons and servants'. The Wednesday 'also was good (about 16 suits), but today we are not so busy which will give time to get straight'. Writing on Thursday 1 December, just four days after receiving the Guest order, Samuel was confident in fulfilling it promptly: 'All their mourning we are sending away by tonight's mails.'

The only problem he had to report was that the company groom, George Neales, had asked to leave: 'he has received a letter (which he showed me) from a foreign gentleman whom he has been in the habit of driving when in London for several seasons'. The foreign gentleman wanted Neales to 'hold himself disengaged' from Poole's, so he would have to go on the Saturday week; but he had promised to find another groom for Henry before then.

Oh, and Jem Mason had called in. Poole's supplied gentlemen not only with clothing but with accessories too, and having ordered some opera glasses, Jem had decided that 'by the bye he would prefer 1 black & 1 white'. Then there had been a visit from a Mr Webb, who had an outstanding balance and 'left the cheques' – not cash – 'for 2nd £200, but talks of wanting to make a good balance' – i.e., settle his account in full – 'on the 23rd.' Samuel enclosed another client's prepared bill, asking Henry to sign and endorse it 'and return by 1st post', and he concluded with affectionate formality, 'We have very cold dry weather here now & seemingly with a prospect of continuance... Hoping you are doing well and enjoying yourself, I remain, Dear Henry, Yrs truly, Samuel Cundey.'

As well as its engaging personal tone, the letter indicates the sheer volume of trade and speed of delivery, which is all the more remarkable given that it was written two full years after the first commercially successful automatic sewing machine, invented by Isaac Merritt Singer, had come on the market. The Singer device could stitch a seam seven times faster than the fastest tailor working by hand, but Henry Poole, a tailor born and bred, disdained it: every garment coming from his workshops continued to be stitched entirely by hand.

The 1850s brought a steady expansion in the company's roll-call of notable customers, including on 3 May 1852 'Mr James Lock, Hatter'. Lock's of St James's Street was (and is) to hats what Poole's was becoming to clothes, and the firm had already measured and fitted such illustrious people as Nelson and the Duke of Wellington. To have Mr Lock's approval must have given Henry particular pleasure, and the two firms still have a friendly relationship.

It was also in the 1850s that Poole's began to gain eminent American clients, starting pretty much at the top of the commercial world with the Morgans. Junius Spencer Morgan began buying in 1854, followed in 1857 by his twenty-year-old

Poole gains a foot-hold in America.
American banker John Pierpont Morgan and other members of his family were among eminent financiers and socialites from across the Atlantic who began to be dressed by Poole.

son the banker, financier and art collector John Pierpont Morgan. Both remained customers for the rest of their lives, as did the Anglophile J. P. Morgan Junior, known as Jack, whose orders included several related to his role as a commodore and ex-commodore of the New York Yacht Club. His last order, in February 1942, was for a blue elastic dinner jacket suit lined with silk, which cost him twenty-three pounds; but perhaps his most notable was his last black silk velvet Court Dress suit. Ordered on 26 May 1937 and made to the pattern established by James Poole in 1839, the complete outfit cost seventy-five pounds and ten shillings, and was returned to the firm each year for pressing – velvet is notoriously difficult to work with. But Jack Morgan died in March 1943 when the suit was back at Henry Poole's for its annual refresher, and unfortunately left no instructions as to what should be done with the garments. Despite their historical interest, they are not on display in the shop: he had become so enormously fat that Poole's has no tailor's dummy large enough. They have therefore been kept carefully in storage ever since, pending instructions for their disposal.

Another of the thousands of items in the Poole collection of the middle nineteenth century is a photograph which was identified during research for this book as being the only known picture of Henry Poole (see page 1). This is an intriguing piece. With glossy, slightly wavy hair neatly parted on the left, the subject is pictured in three-quarters face. Though somewhat thin-lipped, it is a pleasant face, perhaps a little tired: the eyes have slight bags underneath but look ready to light up in smiling. There is no moustache and the chin is clean-shaven, but the subject has impressively huge side-whiskers, and overall he looks to be in his forties. But the photograph is unnamed; so is the subject Henry Poole?

He must be. For one thing, there is no good reason otherwise for the picture to be there; for another, it is one of three separately featuring Henry's cousin Samuel Cundey and Henry's friend Charles Bentley Bingley, and the envelopes containing the pictures are marked 'HGP [Henry George Poole], CBB, SC'. Samuel's portrait is well known in the firm; Bingley's has his initials CBB on it; ergo, the third is Henry.

The picture is undated, but boosting that process of simple elimination, there is also the internal evidence of where it was taken, and by whom. The actual photographer was a G. Jerrard: his printed signature appears on both the front and back of the piece, and he worked in the Claudet studio, supremely fashionable in the early 1850s.

Born in 1797, Jean Francois Antoine Claudet was one of the great early masters of photography: his self-portrait is in the Getty Museum. He was taught by no less a man than Louis Daguerre, inventor of the daguerreotype system, and personally discovered both how to speed up the process so that sitters did not have to maintain a fixed pose for five minutes, and that red light could safely be used while developing pictures. He particularly specialized in stereoscopic images, an early form of three-dimensional photography.

Claudet established his first London studio in 1841, moving in 1851 to 107 Regent Street, which he called the 'Temple to Photography'. Daguerreotypes were still under patent, and Claudet, who owned the rights in England, had only one serious rival, Richard Beard, who used a different method. The profession could be extremely lucrative: Beard charged a guinea (twenty-one shillings) for a head and shoulders portrait, and made eighteen shillings profit on each one. However, it was Claudet who gained royal approval, being appointed 'photographer-in-ordinary' to Queen Victoria in 1853. This was very timely for his studio, because in that same year the Daguerreotype patent – and with it, his effective monopoly – came to an end.

The ostentatious back of the Poole picture carries the Royal Warrant, 'By Appointment to Her Majesty', placing the photograph no earlier than 1853. Similarly, the address of 107 Regent Street places it no later than January 1868, for a rather dramatic reason: Claudet died on 12 December 1867, and within a month the entire Temple to Photography accidentally burned down. All negatives were stored at the studio, and they and many of Claudet's other records were destroyed, making it impossible to give the Poole picture a definite date.

Nevertheless it seems likely that the picture was taken some time in the middle 1850s, and at a guess we might say in late 1854, when Henry had his fortieth birthday. The Claudet studio was conveniently located just around the corner from Savile Row, and the cachet of its Royal Warrant would certainly have appealed to him: what better way for an ambitious gentleman to mark an important birthday than by having his portrait 'taken instantaneously' by the royal photographer?

Shortly after this, in order to match his growing list of customers, Henry began a new stage in the firm's physical growth, buying first the leasehold (and later the freehold in some cases) of buildings adjacent to 38 Savile Row. Between 1856 and 1858 these were extensively and expensively altered to form a continuous suite. It was not difficult to choose a suitable builder (the Cubitts were the best in London, and Josiah Cubitt had been a customer of Poole's since 1846) and in 1858, just about the time when the alterations were being completed, Henry received his first major public accolade: the Imperial Warrant of Napoleon III, Emperor of the French.

What a road had been travelled since 1815 and James Poole's first homemade

The first of many Royal Warrants. The accolade of Louis Napoleon's Warrant in 1858 was the first of an unrivalled 40 Warrants awarded to Henry Poole & Co.

military uniform! Today the emperor's original Warrant still hangs in Poole's show-room, and with its special status as the firm's first, it is displayed in miniature on the company stationery alongside the current Royal Warrant from Her Majesty Queen Elizabeth II: Poole's supply the eye-catching scarlet and gold livery worn on state occasions by the royal household's coachmen, walking grooms and postillions, and each piece is made almost entirely by hand.

Making livery for the servants of noble houses became, in Henry's day, a valu-able part of the company's staple work. Servants were catered for separately from their employers, in a building a few yards up Savile Row on the corner with Clifford Street, and as one memorial of Henry remarked, 'Footmen tricked out by Poole in brimstone and ruby loafed like great golden carp in half the palace entrance halls of Europe, and made the Hyde Park drive from mid-May to July blaze like a bed of Dutch tulips.' Those few summer weeks were the 'London season', the highest point of high society's annual calendar; to miss it, for almost any reason apart from being away for a war or an exploring expedition, was so eccentric as to court social exclu-sion, and Henry made it his duty to ride in Rotten Row every day of the season in the promenading hour, when 'the whole park was a gallery exhibiting his creations.' And along with livery, military uniforms, court dress and fine civilian clothing, the sporting lines were going very well: the author of *The Art of Training Horses*, a book published in 1858, commented that Poole's supplied 'more men and masters of hounds than any tailor, but his customers must be prepared to pay for perfection.'

Returning from the Rotten Row parade to Savile Row, Henry was present in the shop from half past three to five o'clock as the most suave and genial of hosts, providing claret, hock and cigars to clients, apparently without direct charge. Since he was a tailor and not a licensed publican like Samuel Cundey's mother-in-law, of course he could not make a charge on the spot, and in any case that would have spoiled the effect; but with this hospitality it is not surprising that a contemporary newspaper said that 38 Savile Row was 'a great rendezvous for gilded and sporting youth', who treated the premises 'more like a club than a shop'.

In principle Henry could build the cost into customers' bills, but whether he did or not is another question. It is quite possible that this became just another drain on his income – and there still remained the problem of unpaid bills, for the Earl of Mountcashell was far from being the sole offender in that way. In the company ledgers it is all too easy to find examples of prolonged credit and bad debts. Three, picked almost at random from 1860 and 1861, concerned Mr Robert Henry Harper of Upper Tooting, Mr C. Ibbetson of The Grange, Bisham Abbey, and Lord George Townshend of Ashburnham Park, Greenwich.

Mr Harper's case could have been worse. Starting in February 1860, he ordered a superfine black silk-lined lounging coat at five pounds five shillings and sixpence. In the summer he went on to another lounge coat, a waistcoat and a dress coat, and

Royal livery. From Queen Victoria's reign to that of the present monarch, Queen Elizabeth II, Henry Poole & Co have made state livery for the royal coachmen and postillions. Left to right: Full State Footman's Coat 1902; Full State Walking Groom's Coat 1937; Full State Coachman's Coat 1996; Full State Postillion's Coat 1999; Royal Ascot Postillion's Coat 2001

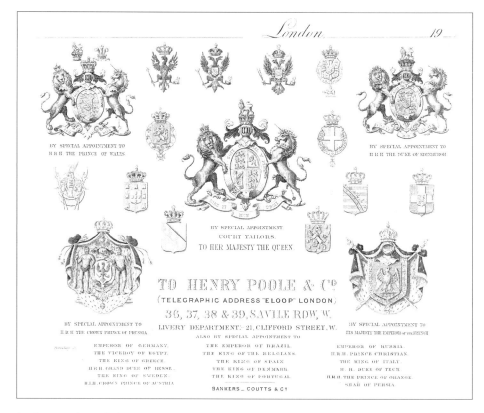

had a number of alterations (new hand facings and buttons) done to a lounge coat. Lastly in the autumn he acquired a cape of brown Elysian ('a heavy wool napped in a wave-like pattern') lined with silk with a velvet collar, and a lounge coat of Oxford thin Melton (Oxford is a dark grey and Melton a mixture of wool and cotton) with silk sleeve linings and a double-sewn waistcoat. The total cost for the year's orders was twenty-five pounds twelve shillings and sixpence, but by the spring of 1862 his unpaid bill had risen to nearly sixty pounds. In March that year he at last paid thirty pounds and fifteen shillings towards it, leaving over twenty-nine pounds carried forward; and of course he immediately went on to order more.

This was all very well if you could be sure that the bill would be paid eventually, but in the interim it meant the firm was effectively required to act as a banker, and that was a situation which – as in the case of Mr Ibbetson – could last for years.

Very little is known about Mr Ibbetson, but it seems he was a pretty fine young man about town. In 1861 he ran up an account of just over one hundred and four pounds, or about £6,250 in 2002 figures. He had good taste: one of his orders was for a superfine green uniform frock coat, braided, with silk skirts and silk sleeve linings at nine guineas; but then on 17 July 1862 he died. The account was passed to a Colonel Ibbeston of 4 Onslow Square, and it is hard to avoid the suspicion that the colonel was his father, who found himself landed with an unexpected and very large bill on his son's behalf. It was not the first time such a thing had happened in the world, and would not be the last, but the colonel was a gentleman of honour: he paid in full and in cash – but not until 9 January 1868.

The last and worst of these three, Lord George Townshend, was introduced as a customer by the Reverend G. Ridsdale. On 11 February 1860 he placed his only set of orders: a cape in fancy mix Witney wool, silk-lined with a velvet collar, a fine silk lounging coat with silk sleeve linings, a silk lounging vest and a pair of brown check buckram trousers, at a total cost of fifteen guineas. Under his entry there is a single, undated word: Bankrupt. The debt remained on the books and on 31 December 1871 was transferred to a new ledger, like the Mountcashell debt.

The contemporary newspaper article describing Henry's 'club' and his generosity with wine and cigars went on to say that 'the firm's well-known trio of high priests, Mr Cundey (General Supervisor), Mr Dent (Coats) and Mr Allen (Trousers) frequently joined the convivial gathering.' Very much later, in the 1950s, another writer hinted that Mr Cundey – Henry's cousin Samuel – and the others must have wondered at Henry's unstinting hospitality, and that Samuel in the late 1860s must have warned him in vain: 'Tell him about the drop in the firm's profits, and his manner became far-off at once.' But there is no written record to prove that, and although Samuel was in a senior position he was not the proprietor. Moreover, there were important parts of Henry's financial affairs that he probably did not know about in detail, if at all, and his decisive actions after Henry's death suggest much more strongly that he was unaware of the time-bombs being made in Savile Row.

Meanwhile Samuel's own life was changing. With increasing prosperity, he and his wife Eliza had moved out of her mother's pub to their first proper home together, 16 Great Castle Street, just north of Oxford Circus and within easy walking distance of the shop. The young couple were beginning a typically large Victorian family: between 1849 and 1869 they had a total of nine children. As the family tree at the back of this book shows, their mortality rate was no less typical of the time: five of the children died in infancy or childhood and two in young adulthood, with only two, Annie and Howard, surviving to middle age and beyond.

By the time Howard was born on 1 June 1857 the family had moved home

Howard Cundey. The cousin who, in 1883, at the age of twenty-six, took on the onerous mantle of managing Henry Poole.

again, to 10 Westbourne Park Road, Paddington, three miles from Savile Row. The area is now overshadowed by a motorway, but its distance from Samuel's work is another sign of increasing prosperity, since he would probably not have walked every day but would have driven in a carriage. On Howard's birth certificate Samuel is described as a 'master tailor', and despite the early deaths of some of his children, in his middle thirties his life was tolerably good by contemporary standards. But sometimes it is fortunate the future cannot be foretold, because, as we shall see, cousin Henry's reckless pursuit of the life of a gentleman cost many people dear – and it probably cost Samuel his life.

CHAPTER 7

Happiness, Pride and Disaster

For Henry Poole, the 1860s were a glowing decade in which it seemed nothing could go wrong in either his personal or his business life. On 10 February 1859 at the village church in Lee, near Lewisham in what is now south-east London, he had married Emma Walker, the daughter of a draper. She had been one of his employees, supervisor of the section dealing with ladies' riding habits, and it must have been a love-match: she is reputed to have had little or no dowry, and while Henry was forty-four at the time of the wedding, she was forty-one, so there was no real prospect of children. Ceasing her paid work on marriage, Emma came to live at Dorset Cottage, where the 1861 census recorded a total of eleven souls: Henry, Emma, Henry's aged mother Mary (she was eighty-four), his never-to-be-married sister Mary Ann, Emma's older unmarried sister Eliza and younger brother Thomas (an upholsterer), Henry's step-niece Fanny Walton, and, looking after them all, four unnamed female servants.

It was also in 1859 that the expansion of business induced Henry to buy the leasehold of workshops at 65 King Street (now Kingly Street) in Soho, just the other side of Regent Street – usefully close to Savile Row, yet far enough away to mean that customers did not have to see his workers' conditions. But the event which launched the 1860s for him was a night at the theatre. The play starred a French actor named Charles Fechter in the role of an adventurer, and in the audience was Queen Victoria's eldest son, the eighteen-year-old Edward, then Prince of Wales and subsequently King Edward VII. Many years later, Edward's grandson the Duke of Windsor told the outcome of the theatricals simply enough:

> *The adventurer's coat, in the piece, was a mass of rents and patches, but the acute royal eye quickly noticed that the garment was well cut, and at the end of the play he [Prince Edward] sent for the actor and asked him for the name of his tailor. The answer was Poole…*

Acting is such a precarious profession that it sounds improbable for an actor to have his stage clothes made to measure by a tailor whose customers even then had to be 'prepared to pay for perfection', and an investigation of the company ledgers shows that whereas Fechter was a paying client from 11 April 1861, the Prince of Wales placed his first order in 1860. Thus it seems most likely that Henry, with his ear to the

Edward, Prince of Wales placed his first order with Henry Poole in 1860 and from then on Poole's became the Prince's chief tailor.

55

commercial ground, knew in advance of the prince's visit to the theatre and had initially clothed the actor for free, just as his father had clothed him and he had clothed Jem Mason. In any event, the clothes themselves were once again the firm's best advertisement, and the Duke of Windsor's conclusion was accurate: 'from that day Poole became the Prince's chief tailor.'

After Henry's lifetime this proved to be a poisoned chalice, because although the prince and his friends in 'the Marlborough House set' ordered copiously, he was perfectly prepared to allow them very long – indeed, interminable – credit. Many ordinary fathers would think it an act of insanity to offer a teenager unlimited credit for a clothing budget, but Henry Poole was not and never would be a father, and Prince Edward was not an ordinary teenager. At the time it seemed simply that Henry had secured one of the best of all possible customers, and his crop of prominent clients increased still further: among others joining the list that year were the Prince of Liechtenstein, Prince Nicholas Troubitzkoy, Grand Duke Michael of Russia, the great hotelier William Claridge, and Benjamin Disraeli, former chancellor of the Exchequer and later prime minister of Great Britain.

Disraeli was a good novelist as well as a politician, and in his last book (*Endymion*, first published in 1880) there is a character based on Henry. Vigo Street connects Glasshouse Street and Savile Row, and Disraeli's Mr Vigo was 'the most fashionable tailor in London … consummate in his art … neither pretentious nor servile, but simple, and with becoming respect for others and for himself'. These were the qualities which enabled Henry to consort easily with so many of his social superiors, who now were practically queuing up to get on his books – new customers in 1861 included Grand Duke Constantine of Russia, Archduke Maximilian of Austria (who as the puppet Emperor of Mexico was shot dead six years later), the Crown Prince of Germany, and a greater novelist than Disraeli: Charles Dickens himself, who died in 1870 owing Henry money.

The client list rapidly took on the air of some kind of fairytale or fantasy as more and more exotic names were added: in 1862 came the novelist Wilkie Collins, followed by the King of the Belgians, Prince Mustapha Pasha of Egypt, Grand Duke Frederic of Baden, and General Lord Cardigan, leader of the disastrous charge of the Light Brigade at Balaclava; then in

Charles Dickens and other literati come onto the books at Henry Poole. A copy of Charles Dickens's cheque of 1865 is still on display at their premises today.

Eminent clients from all sectors of society. Politicians such as Prime Minister Benjamin Disraeli (left) and author Wilkie Collins (centre).

A short-lived imperial customer. Archduke Maximilian of Austria (right) became a Poole customer in 1861, was appointed Emperor of Mexico in 1863, and executed in 1867.

1863, the Prince of Orange, Prince Metternich, the Duke of Edinburgh (Prince Edward's brother), the King of Greece, King Christian of Denmark (Prince Edward's father-in-law) and Crown Prince Humbert of Italy; in 1864, another great novelist, Anthony Trollope, and the Emperor of Russia; and in 1865, the King of Portugal, Prince Christian of Holstein, Prince Frederick of Prussia (Prince Edward's brother-in-law), the Grand Duke of Saxe Weimar, the Duke of Aosta, Napoleon III's chief ranger the Baron de Wimpferen, the librettist W. S. Gilbert of Gilbert and Sullivan (who may well have found inspiration in this extraordinary clientele), and by no means least, Prince Edward's mother, Queen Victoria herself. Prince Edward had married in 1863, wearing a uniform made for the occasion by Poole's, and now the queen ordered a blue milled beaver braid-trimmed overcoat lined with moleskin for her daughter-in-law, together with a blue fur overcoat with silk velvet collar for Prince Christian. Including a three-shilling charge for a packing case, the garments cost fourteen pounds seventeen shillings, or about £890 in modern terms. (The bill was paid in full in February 1868, more than two years after delivery, yet when the queen died in 1901, her other orders left twelve shillings and sixpence outstanding, still unpaid today; but the company has waived the charge.)

Three other new clients in 1865 deserve a note: William C. Whitney, Evander Berry Wall and Catherine 'Skittles' Walters. Whitney and Wall were both American; Whitney was the Secretary of State for the Navy, the company's first US Government client, and ordered a dahlia-coloured velvet beaver frock coat, with velvet cuffs and lapels. Wall had a bizarre claim to fame as the 'King of the Dudes': in the course of one afternoon he managed to strut around his hotel in Saratoga Springs in no fewer than forty different suits, all made by Henry Poole & Company. It is said that next day this phenomenon was in all the newspapers, coast to coast.

The most celebrated 'kept mistress' of the Victorian age. Catherine 'Skittles' Walters' skin-tight riding habits were a living advertisement for Henry Poole's tailoring skills and even prompted letters to The Times and Daily Telegraph.

Catherine Walters was something else, in every way. Born in 1839, she was known as Skittles because as a little girl she had worked in a skittle alley in a pub in Liverpool. She grew up to be extremely beautiful, an expert horse-woman and the most celebrated 'kept mistress' of the Victorian age. Moving to London (and before becoming the mistress of the Marquis of Hartington, with a life settlement of two thousand pounds a year), she found a job with the owner of a stables and became a living advertisement for his horses, riding them or driving a carriage in Hyde Park. She also became a living advertisement for Henry Poole's riding habits. Seated side-saddle for her fittings on his artificial horse Bucephalus, she was provided with a skin-tight habit which was so perfectly shaped to her figure that eventually there were letters in *The Times* and *Daily Telegraph*: the crowds who streamed out to watch her ride were regularly blocking the roads, so could 'this pretty creature and her pretty ponies' not be persuaded to exercise somewhere else?

This was not Henry's only method of blocking roads, getting into the press and generally making Poole & Company memorable. Prince Edward granted Poole's his Royal Warrant in 1863, and soon the portico of 38 Savile Row was permanently decorated with a giant version of his coat of arms, while above it, whenever the Emperor and Empress of the French came to visit, there was a stupendously large imperial eagle flanked by their initials, crowns and tricolours, with the whole display being illuminated at night from inside and out by gas flares. Similar spectacles were set out on every occasion of royal celebration. These illuminations would be a remarkable sight even today, when the streets hold so much neon and artificial light; then, they were sensational, and people who saw them never forgot them. In 1863, when Prince Edward married, a fifteen-year-old youth went with a party of friends in a hired omnibus to see Poole's display; in November 1865, carried on her father's shoulders, a four-year-old girl saw the gas-lit exhibition for the prince's twenty-fourth birthday; and in 1935 at the silver jubilee of King George V, both these onlookers (by then aged eighty-seven and seventy-four respectively) still remembered vividly those illuminations of long ago, recollecting not only the beauty but the immense crowds – Regent Street was so congested that the young man's hired omnibus was stuck in one position for nearly an hour.

At this point the story of Henry Poole & Co must enter an area of some international controversy: the origin of the dinner jacket or tuxedo. In 1986 the

American Formalwear Association celebrated the garment's alleged centenary, asserting that short jackets of this type were first worn (in preference to the standard formal tail-coat for gentlemen's evening wear) in October 1886 by twenty-two-year-old Griswold Lorillard, heir to a tobacco company, and several of his friends at a formal ball in the Tuxedo Club in New York's Tuxedo Park. However, although the Club can undoubtedly stake rightful claim to the origin of the American name for the garment, 'Grizzy's' coat was not a dinner jacket at all. Worn for a joke, it was a tail coat with the tails cut off, looking something like a mess jacket. (It was recorded that Grizzy looked 'for all the world like a royal footman', and that onlookers felt he and his friends 'ought to have been put in strait-jackets long ago.') Moreover, there are other named contenders for the origin of the dinner jacket, including a second from the Tuxedo Club, a New York financier named James Brown Potter. Another is Evander Berry Wall, 'King of the Dudes', who is said to have worn such a jacket three months earlier in Saratoga and was summarily ejected from the formal event. A French source says that the first wearers were the players at the casino in Monte Carlo, who in 1880 refused to continue wearing tails and chose the new

The great showman. Enormous crowds were attracted to Henry Poole's dramatic gas-lit display on the front of his premises. On this occasion, it was to celebrate the state visit to London of his client Emperor Louis Napoleon III of France.

short style, *le smoking*, instead; and the same source states that other people insist the style originated in Germany, and that it was brought from there to Britain by Lord Dupplin towards the end of the nineteenth century.

Among three of the named individuals above (Lorillard, Wall and Dupplin) there is one glaringly obvious common factor: all were customers of Henry Poole, Lorillard from 1885, Wall from 1865 and Dupplin from as long ago as 1848. What, then, does Poole's say about the matter? Simply this: that it started when the Prince of Wales commissioned a short smoking jacket from the company in 1865, a garment so informal that it was very much for private use. In 1886 the prince met James Brown Potter, took a liking to his beautiful wife Cora and invited them to stay for the weekend at Sandringham, his country home, advising Potter that he always wore short coats in the evening. Potter only had the customary tail-coat for evening wear, so consulted Poole's, who promptly made him the necessary attire; and given that it had the royal imprimatur, Brown wore it later in Tuxedo.

Potter's name has not been found in Poole's books, so the argument cannot be said to be completely settled; but overall it seems that when it comes to the dinner jacket, most roads lead to Poole's, whoever may have first worn it in the United States. The paradox is that a garment which began its existence as an almost scandalously informal piece is nowadays regarded by many as the epitome of smart formality.

Going back now to the 1860s, Henry Poole's fairytale existence continued with only two recorded interruptions. In 1862 his mother died – a sad event, but not unexpected, given her age. The other interruption was unexpected. Henry had taken to having annual autumn holidays in France with his friends the emperor and empress, and in the midst of one of those vacations, in 1866, he received an urgent message: the workforce of London tailors was threatening to go on strike.

The protagonists in this affair were the employers' union the Master Tailors' Association, of which Henry was chairman, and the workers' union, the Operative Tailors' Protective Association. The issue between them was the level of pay for non-salaried 'journeymen' tailors, men and women taken on when business was brisk in spring and summer. Under the existing strictly piecework system their pay worked out at about sixpence an hour – not generous, but when compared to other workers' pay, not particularly mean either. However, it was not guaranteed, the seasonality of the work was a difficulty, and before his holiday, Henry (who had about four hundred non-salaried workers) had been asked to increase prices so as to give them sevenpence an hour. Through the Master Tailors' Association he had responded with a new 'log', the amount paid for each garment, and while he was away the Operative Tailors calculated this would leave people worse off than before – hence the threatened strike of two thousand of their members.

Henry's first reaction, and that of the other Master Tailors, was to bully. Sending out a call for further journeymen from all over Europe, the Master Tailors organized a lock-out of the journeymen at home. The stand-off continued for ten days, until it became clear that the workers' association was more influential than anticipated by the masters: the foreign journeymen did not appear. Compromise became essential, and Henry produced a new formula which his workers (and soon afterwards, the others) accepted. The piecework principal remained for traditional hand-stitching, but now with a guaranteed minimum of sixpence an hour, and two sewing machines were brought into the workshop for stitching linings. Work with these would be paid at half the hand-stitching rate, but because the machines were so much faster there would be a net gain for the workers.

Thus the matter was settled, at least for the time being. It is perhaps worth repeating that by contemporary standards these modest rates of pay were not as exploitative as they sound. But it was an exploitative and extremely unequal society, and the figures emphasise the gulf between the people who made the clothes and those who wore them.

As Henry garnered other prestigious clients (Prince Hermann of Hohenlohe Langenburg in 1866, the fourth Earl of Rosebery in 1867, the Duke of Genoa in 1868), he became still more ambitious. In 1866 this led him into a small amount of trouble with one of his neighbours, William Johnson of 19 Clifford Street. The freehold of Johnson's property and of Henry's at 37 Savile Row belonged to the Pollen Estate, a large Mayfair landowning trust, and the two properties shared a party wall. Johnson's complaint was that Henry's 'alterations, additions and improvements' had encroached on this, and he insisted that 'said encroachments shall not in any manner abridge prejudice or affect' his own rights. Being entirely in the wrong, Henry agreed quickly, even accepting that if Johnson chose at any time to make any improvements himself or take down Henry's then he, Henry, would pay for the changes. Typically, the only person to benefit from the spat was Johnson's lawyer, who sent Henry a bill for more than nine pounds.

Ownership was the best way round such irritations, and in 1866 Henry acquired 20 and 21 Clifford Street, rebuilding them as single premises. These were on leasehold, as was his new home: in 1866, while retaining Dorset Cottage, he bought the lease to 118 Marine Parade in Brighton, the house in which just ten years later he would die. He went further in London too, acquiring in 1867 the lease of 36 Savile Row; but every tenant, especially in London, knows that leasehold is almost as nothing compared to freehold, and in 1868 Henry decided to buy the freehold not only of his extended premises at 38 Savile Row, but also of the adjacent 37 Savile Row and 5 Old Burlington Street, next door to his father's first Mayfair premises at number 4, which was now regarded as separate to number 38 and remained on lease. Finally in 1869 he acquired the leasehold of 3 Old Burlington Street and 39 Savile Row, and his property empire was complete.

The Khedive of Egypt proved how extensive the geographical range of Henry Poole's clients was, and still is.

To crown all this (almost literally), further Royal and Imperial Warrants flowed in: in 1869 those of the King of the Belgians, the Crown Prince of Denmark and Queen Victoria; in 1870, from the Khedive of Egypt and the Prince of Teck; in 1871, from King Amadeus of Spain, Prince Oscar of Sweden and Norway, and Prince Louis of Hesse; and in 1874 the last that he personally would receive, from the Emperor of Brazil. But then came a personal disaster: on 2 September 1870 at Sedan in north-east France, Emperor Napoleon III of France was defeated after forty-four days of war with King Wilhelm of Prussia, now Kaiser of a newly united Germany. France became a republic again, and although still valued and valuable, Napoleon's Warrant – Henry's first – was suddenly and decisively consigned to history.

CHAPTER 8

A Monstrous Proceeding

After the calamity of Napoleon's defeat, another came hard on its heels: FIRE AT POOLE'S, said *The Tailor and Cutter* – COMPLETE DESTRUCTION OF THE SHOPS IN KING STREET. On Friday 28 October 1870 gas fittings had been installed in the workshops, but were 'left in an insecure condition'. The blaze began at nine that evening, and despite the fire brigade's prompt response it took nearly an hour to subdue the flames. About a hundred men worked there, and all their personal property and garments in making ('of considerable value') were destroyed. There is no record to say whether the building and contents were insured, but 'we believe', said the magazine, 'that it is not the intention of Mr Poole to rebuild'. However, there was quick action to ensure continued production: twenty-five of the men were found temporary work space in 'the bottom shop', which 'was not so much destroyed' (but which must have been a dreadful place to work, with the lingering stench of the fire) and on the following Wednesday the entire work force was moved to emergency premises in nearby Heddon Street.

Despite these serious setbacks there was no slackening of the tide of distinguished new customers, including Britain's most famous contemporary explorer David Livingstone (who took on his African expeditions a belted poncho, forerunner of the raincoat, made by Poole's), Lord Randolph Churchill, the Duke of Connaught, Prince Frederic of Hohenlohe, and in 1876 (of all imaginable people) Prince Bismarck – Germany's 'Iron Chancellor', the man who had engineered the Franco-Prussian war and had directly negotiated with Napoleon III on the terms of France's surrender. The site of that event may well have had a special poignancy for Henry Poole: the negotiation took place in a tiny cottage belonging to a weaver.

Yet by far the most interesting and unusual of Henry's new clients were two other princes: His Highness Prince Taschimi Mitzumo Miya and HH Prince Higashi Fushimino Miya, who became customers in 1871 together with Mr A. Shioda. This gave Henry Poole & Co a supreme historical privilege, because the princes were not only members of the Japanese imperial household but also

The Iron Chancellor. After defeating the French in the Franco-Prussian war and personally negotiating France's terms of surrender with Napoleon III, ironically, Prince Bismarck himself became a customer of Poole's.

Recognition by the Japanese Imperial Household. As a result of Poole's long-standing Japanese connections, in 1923 they were awarded the highest of accolades when granted the Imperial Warrant.

of the first embassy from Japan to the West, of which Shioda was First Secretary. Moreover the connection led in 1923 to the award of the Warrant of the Imperial Household, and in 1964 it gained further commercial strength when a long-standing association was formalized between Poole's and the prestigious Matsuzakaya chain. Established in 1611, Matsuzakaya is Japan's oldest retail organization, and their licensing agreement – still very much alive – is one of the oldest in existence between Great Britain and Japan.

But if the 1860s had been a golden period in Henry's lifetime, the 1870s – his last years – were its most critical. It is hard now to assess the extent of the effect upon him of Napoleon's defeat, but he and the French court were so intimately connected that the blow was certainly very severe, and coming so swiftly afterwards, the fire at King Street would only have added to his worries. By no means did everything go wrong for him: apart from anything else, he was awarded the Warrant of the Emperor of Russia in 1875, and of the Emperor of Germany. However, it has been said that from 1870 to 1874 he was scarcely in the shop. This may be true, and it may be that after the fall of the French imperial court he attempted to engage in other business: the 1871 census records him (in what would have been his own description) as a 'broker and merchant', but without saying what kind of brokering this was.

What is certain is that by 1871 he had reduced his household in Brighton to himself, his wife Emma and his sister Mary Ann (with, it should be added, four female servants and two manservants), and that in April 1872 he undertook a review of the values of all his freehold and leasehold property, including the surrender value of a life insurance policy. This seems to have been the first time he ever did such an exercise, and it revealed some shocking information.

The total value of his real estate was £33,750 (about two million sterling in 2002 figures), two-thirds being in the freeholds of Dorset Cottage, 5 Old Burlington Street, and 37 and 38 Savile Row. Superficially the situation was healthy; but there were some grave drawbacks. His other properties, the leaseholds, were all short-term: nothing like the 999-year leases that may be found on new buildings today, or even the sixty-year opening leases that Lord Burlington placed on 'Savile Street' and the rest in the 1730s. Instead, one of Henry's leases would have to be renewed at a new rate in 1877 and another in 1883, and even the longest ran only until 1890.

Worse: his purchase and improvements of Dorset Cottage had cost him an estimated £16,000, but the property was valued at only £10,000. Worse still:

against the freeholds in Old Burlington Street and Savile Row there was a mortgage of £16,000 (about a million sterling in 2002 figures), taken out when he bought them in 1868. Annual interest was four per cent, with the principal repayable on 3 November 1877.

In other words, approximately one-third of his real estate was in short-term leasehold (by definition a declining asset); he had spent far more on Dorset Cottage than it was worth; and of the other freeholds, valued at £22,700 in money of the day, £16,000 would be taken up in redeeming the mortgage – assuming the interest had been paid.

As we know, financial discipline was not Henry's forte, and the mortgage was not with a bank or similar institution but with two private individuals, William Bligh O'Connell and Gerald Surman. If (like Henry with so many of his customers) they had been content to let the debt lie on their books gathering interest, then by its redemption date in 1877 the principal and cumulative interest would add up to £23,380 – about £1.4 million in modern terms, and more than the freeholds' estimated value.

Whether he had been paying the interest or not, this was a dire situation. The short-term leaseholds could be ignored as a long-term benefit to his estate. Leaving them aside, the plain fact was that when the mortgage redemption date arrived, he would have to find either the modern equivalent of about a million pounds (the principal) or, if cumulative interest were unpaid, possibly much more. The first would reduce him considerably; the second could break him.

Henry seems to have been able to think of only one solution: two notes in the company archives show that on 17 June 1872, seven weeks after his financial review, he took out another loan, for a massive £22,000 at five per cent interest. There is no further detail, but this may have been to pay off the earlier one. There is a hint too that he began trying to call in debts, charging more than expected: a letter dated 25 June 1875 from the secretary of the fifth Earl of Rosebery (grandson of Henry's earlier customer the fourth earl) brought a cheque for £133, including a payment of £80 for a velvet dress –

"Poole's, I presume?" An alternative version of Stanley's famous question to Dr Livingstone – both of whom were clients. But this imaginative contemporary fashion plate shows them wearing clothes more suitable for London than Africa.

El Demi Dess Paris

Imp Lemercier & C.ie de Seine S.t Paris

" D.r Livingstone I presume ! "

about £4,800 in modern money. But the price had not been discussed at the time of ordering, and Rosebery's secretary wrote that the angry earl

> *did not know why it should cost more than the dress which he gave to Lady Caroline Villiers, and which certainly cost less than £80. He considers the spending of £80 of his money without a word of warning being addressed to him as a monstrous proceeding.*

A not unreasonable reaction, one might say, and Rosebery decided to order no more from Poole's – which was particularly unfortunate, because he was very influential: not only a successful sporting man, whose horses won the Derby three times, but also a rising politician who would one day be prime minister.

Keeping a record of his customers' weights. In 1875 Henry Poole installed jockey scales and a record book for his customers in his showroom. They are still on display today.

Then there was the matter of the jockey scales, installed in Henry's showroom around this time (and still there). From his long-standing love of racing Henry would have been familiar with the device, but it was installed because he had 'a dispute with a customer' over the payment for letting out a costly uniform. The same note in the archives adds: 'The customer denied that he had put on weight but Mr Poole thought otherwise. A book was kept beside the scales and contains many distinguished names. The first entry was in April, 1875.' No doubt most of those who were weighed thought it a fine joke, all part of Old Pooley's style, and today the scales seem quaint and amusing; but they are also another sign of his unaccustomed sensitivity about money and the mental anguish he was experiencing, because normally speaking, Henry ('consummate in his art … neither pretentious nor servile, but simple, and with becoming respect for others and for himself', as Disraeli wrote) would never have argued with a client.

Another note from 1875 indicates that sales for the previous year had totalled £182,000, with gross profits of £47,600 – by today's standards, an unacceptably low margin of only twenty-six per cent. Stock was valued at £19,000, 'good' book debts at £137,000, and liabilities at £76,000. By then Henry was ill: a letter of 18 June 1875, beginning 'Mr Poole being still very poorly has asked me to reply', was written on his behalf by his friend Charles Bingley. When Henry died on 4 May 1876 two causes of death were given: a state of apoplexy (a stroke) which had lasted ten hours before he expired, and a 'contracted kidney', from which he had suffered for two years, that is, since 1874. The stroke was not his first – 'For some time past', said one of his obituaries, 'he had been subject to apoplectic fits and had become much depressed' – and from the medical diagnoses it seems likely that the combination of circumstances from late 1870 (the fall of Napoleon and the fire) to early

1872 (the financial review) brought about a state of utter despair; indeed it may be that the greatest tailor in the world went (in tailors' slang) 'on the cod' and began to drink very heavily.

The last surviving letter he ever wrote is dated 'Friday evening 8 Octo' and was sent from his Brighton address to Bingley, who had agreed to be his sole executor. He did not give a year date on the letter, but it was certainly written in 1875 (8 October 1875 was a Friday). Disjointed, rambling, ungrammatical and almost completely unpunctuated, it shows a man who was in a far from normal state of mind. But towards its end come two tragically clear sentences:

> *The trouble will not be what you thought – There will be nothing much to leave behind me. I have worked for a prince and for the public & must die a poor man – and less trouble to Executor.*

We shall return to this shortly. The archives contain another letter, the last surviving one that Henry ever received. Dated 23 April 1876, soon after his fateful phaeton drive in the unseasonable snow-storm in Brighton, it was addressed from the Prince of Wales Theatre in Liverpool. The irony cannot have been lost on him: it had been that visit by the Prince of Wales to a London theatre in 1860 which had launched him on the most majestic phase of his career. The writer was an actor, clearly on good terms with Henry, a debtor of his, and no better than he at managing finances. 'My dear Poole,' he wrote,

> *Once more upon the stormy path of my eventful life have I found a resting place. My success has been tremendous, and I don't think you will be the last to wish me well. It is hard for a man at my time of life to have to go play-acting, but with the load of my debts still hanging round my neck like a millstone which I have never been able to clear off, I could not let so golden an opportunity pass.*
>
> *Now I want to pay off as fast as I can, and when I come to London, which will be when I have finished my engagement here, I shall come and see you & talk over the matter. I open at the Olympic on the 15th of May and I want you to send all your men into the pit and the gallery to give me a reception.*

But this promise of payment from a fellow debtor carried a sting in the tail: Henry's men would not be given free entry to the theatre. 'If you'll send Neville [the theatre manager] a check it would be better… Dear Poole, ever yours…' Receiving the letter just three days before he died, Henry can only have read it with the hollowest of hollow laughs.

From Coronation robes to footmen's buttons. The ninth Duke of Marlborough ordered extensively from Henry Poole and was conspicuous for paying promptly.

There is much that will never be known for certain about the life and character of Henry Poole. It is possible that for most of his life he was simply a most tremendous optimist, believing like Mr Micawber that 'something will turn up'; and with his deep-seated love of horses and the sporting life he may have had the gambler's belief that all would come right with the next winner in. However, in the detailed list of his properties' values, the balance sheet of his real estate was laid down in simple figures, and if (as seems likely) he commissioned it himself, then at least he was not entirely self-deceptive. But how much of this information did he share with his dependants, his sister Mary Ann and their cousin Samuel Cundey? There is nothing to indicate that he let them know the extent of his debts compared to the appearance of his wealth; rather, the evidence is that after his death, the revelation was a thunderbolt. Was he really so duplicitous? Was his life a sham, a handsome façade like his Savile Row premises? These questions are unanswerable.

Unanswerable too is the question of how his last surviving letter out was read by its addressee Charles Bingley. An executor's task can be onerous and time-consuming, and Bingley had clearly expressed doubts about taking it on: Henry wrote to him, 'The trouble will not be what you thought', adding as an explanation, 'There will be nothing much to leave behind me... and less trouble to Executor.' Bingley might have read this as a becomingly modest assessment. But Henry was right about one thing: 'the trouble' that followed his death was not what Bingley, or Mary Ann, or Samuel Cundey thought it would be.

CHAPTER 9

The Burial of the Dead

Henry's Will was very long: fourteen pages of text, closely written and tortuously expressed. In it, he left half his business to his cousin Samuel Cundey and a quarter to his step-niece Fanny Cutler (her husband Edwin, another tailor, was the person who had attended his dying days and had forwarded his farewell to the Prince of Wales). The fourth quarter of the business and his half-interest in 171 Regent Street were left to his executor and trustee Charles Bingley, 'in recognition and acknowledgement of his kindness in undertaking the management of my business at considerable personal sacrifice at a time when from indisposition I became unable to attend to the management thereof myself'.

The Will's other most important elements were that Henry acknowledged and promised to repay a debt of £3,000 to his sister Mary Ann and left the same amount to his widow Emma, as well as a generous annuity for each of them: £2,500 apiece, or about £150,000 in modern figures. But there were conditions attached to the bequests: firstly, Mary Ann was expressly forbidden to force payment of the £3,000 debt, on pain of forfeiting her annuity. Secondly, there was no actual cash for any of this: everything was to be funded from the outright sale or future profits of the business, which Bingley was to run 'to the best advantage', but 'without any obligation to bestow more time and attention to it than he in his absolute discretion shall think fit' – and Henry 'earnestly' requested Samuel Cundey and Fanny Cutler not to interfere with Bingley in its management.

There was no tidy capability of delivering those well-meant annuities: in effect, his beneficiaries had to rely on Bingley to generate the benefits. Henry appears to have stayed in his financial dream-world to the very end.

He died on a Thursday. His Will was soon read, and on the following Tuesday, 9 May, the day before his burial, his solicitor wrote to Samuel Cundey. It was a most poignant letter:

My dear Sir,

Mr Poole by his Will gives his watches, jewels, ornaments of the person and wearing apparel to Mrs Poole, in addition to which he authorizes Mr Bingley to give to her and Miss Poole or either of them such portions of the furniture and personal household effects as Mr Bingley in his discretion might think fit. I have spoken to him about this. It places him in rather an invidious position as to the

H.R.H. The Prince of Wales

Edward, Prince of Wales. Henry Poole's long term client, and to whom he sent a farewell message from his deathbed.

Numbers 36–39 Savile Row. From 1846 to 1961 some of the most eminent people in the world passed through these doors to be fitted out by Henry Poole & Co. (Originally it was number 32 but shortly after Henry moved in the whole of Savile Row was renumbered.)

selection, and he is anxious to do nothing on that point without consulting you and Mr Cutler. My own opinion is that having regard to the monetary position in which Mr Poole has left his business it would be unwise and, I might add, improper for Mr Bingley to appropriate to Mrs and Miss Poole the furniture and other household effects. This observation of course applies to the bulk and not to any few articles which Mrs or Miss Poole might express a wish to have and which Mr Bingley would be willing to concede, but he does not feel in a position to do more, and the very object of the discretion being vested in him was that he might act according to the circumstances which might exist at the time of Mr Poole's death. You know what they are…

By now Samuel did know, all too well. The letter continued:

…the Estate cannot afford anything more to be done, having regard both to the large amount of outstanding debts due from the Estate and to the necessity of providing by every means in Mr Bingley's power for those debts and for the annuities…

Charles Bingley. Henry Poole's friend and sole executor, who was left to unravel his complicated financial affairs.

Emma and Mary Ann were not even entitled to retain their furniture, apart from 'any few articles' that Bingley might 'concede'. In one way Henry's wish to ensure their financial comfort is touching; but his total lack of realism must have been infuriating too, because for all the good his wishes did, he might as well have willed them a million pounds a day. It was the last and ultimate contrast between him and his father, and it is easy to imagine his mourners' conflicting emotions as they stood by the family grave in Highgate and watched his coffin being interred.

'It is not given to many public men', said the *Sporting Gazette*, 'to create such sincere regret in high circles by their death as, I fancy, it has been to Mr Poole.' Another obituary observed that Henry had been 'very natty as to his carriages, and gave high prices for harness horses.' Now it was left to the family to pick up the bill somehow; and they did, but it took several years and several lives.

Surrounded by iron railings and located three graves in from a steep path that becomes muddy in wet weather, the Poole grave then displayed a tall column. Today half the column has fallen, the victim of vandals or time; its broken pieces push through the railings and ivy obscures much of the whole, a symbol of what might have become of Henry Poole & Co. According to family tradition, that fate was avoided largely because of the efforts of Mary Ann and Samuel Cundey: the story handed down is that Mary Ann refused to see the firm wound up and gave her half-share in the rents of 171 Regent Street towards its recovery. The property's leasehold remained as a family and business asset until its sale in 1898. Moreover, despite the wording of Henry's Will, there is no evidence that Bingley actually ran the business, but rather that Samuel did, as its half-owner.

Among the black-edged letters of condolence that flowed in to Savile Row, one stands out. Dated 10 July 1876, it was abrupt and to the point, which was not to express sympathy:

Another spectacular Poole's façade. This one was to celebrate the wedding of Edward Prince of Wales and Princess Alexandra of Denmark in 1863.

71

Mr Condy [sic]

Can you lend me £300 for a week until I can draw it out of the Westminster bank next Monday?

    If you can do so conveniently will you send it to me in notes between eleven & twelve tomorrow?

    I am, Yours faithfully…

How Samuel reacted is not recorded, but the letter was worth preserving, if only for its audacious insensitivity at a time when sales and private economizing were the order of the day. The archives do not list when the unexpired lease of 118 Marine Parade was sold, but it was. Nor do they list the date of the sale of Dorset Cottage in Fulham, but a year before his death Henry had been negotiating with a Colonel Lewis Guy Philips for the sale of a portion of that estate, and in due course it all went, to be covered over in later years by an oil company's storage tanks.

Inside Poole's. The showroom was considered even more elegant than the exterior.

The ladies moved into number 71 Onslow Gardens, and the contents of Henry's homes were put up for sale. One of the saddest archive items is the catalogue of his collection of watercolours and engravings, annotated by hand with prices achieved. Auctioned at Christie's on Saturday, 24 February 1877, there were eighty-five lots reflecting his tastes: coastal scenes, rivers, sea ports, lakes, cathedrals, sporting scenes. Two which must have had a particular significance for him were a signed artist's proof engraving of *The Derby Day* and a chromo-lithograph of *The Mistress of the Buckhounds*, the hunt to which he and Jem Mason had supplied fresh horses in the middle 1840s. Buyers did not rate those ones highly: the Derby Day picture went for six guineas and the Buckhounds for only one pound five shillings. But at the other end of the scale, the most expensive was a watercolour by Thomas Miles Richardson (1784-1848) entitled *The Bay of Naples: Midday Rest*, which was sold for 154 guineas – and its buyer was Samuel Cundey.

The art sale realized just over £2,239 (about £134,000 in 2002 figures). The records of the sales of the French furniture and the violin collection have not survived, but they went too, and after less than a year of this dreadful strain – and no doubt shame as well – Henry's widow Emma died, on 2 May 1877. On Wednesday 8 May, just two days short of the first anniversary of Henry's interment, she joined him in the Highgate grave. And not even that was family property any more: on 25 November 1876 its ownership had been transferred to Charles Bingley, who by then must have profoundly regretted agreeing to be Henry's executor. 'The trouble will not be what you thought' – no, indeed.

Samuel Cundey and his family were also directly affected. He and Eliza now had four children, Annie (twenty-five), Howard (nineteen), Joseph (sixteen) and Oliver (fourteen). All had moved back into 5 Old Burlington Street, Samuel's final address. Although he would have been paying the rent on the former family home, 10 Westbourne Park Road, from his salary, and in principle could have continued to do so, the move may have been so that he could live rent-free and draw a lower salary. At the same time he set about the recovery of as many as possible of the sums owed to the firm. The Prince of Wales paid up, though apparently not very promptly and in considerable chagrin, then withdrew his custom. However, unrecoverable debts are said to have amounted to £10,000 – six hundred thousand or so in modern terms. With such ageing debts as that of Lord Mountcashell for his own clothes and his daughters' riding habits, you would not need many defaulting customers to reach so painfully large a sum.

The artificial horse Bucephalus was disposed of and the firm ceased to make ladies' riding habits. The Empress Elizabeth of Austria and her sister ex-Queen Marie of Naples, 'those two outsize Dianas', were among the last to be so supplied. Otherwise normal trading continued, albeit with some fall-off: gross profits slipped from a peak of over £184,000 in 1874 to a low of under £142,000 in 1879; and not every customer was happy. In May 1879 one called Clarence Trelawny wrote in asperity from Germany, saying,

> *Gentlemen,*
>
> *Herewith I enclose check for £9.4 – which I do with anything but pleasure, as the things you last sent me convince me that there is no longer that <u>care</u> and <u>attention</u> paid to my clothes that existed in former years.*
>
> *The coat sleeves [are] much too short, and it hangs very badly in front. The trousers [are] too tight round the waist & too tight between the legs. The latter have been altered but the tailor in Frankfurt informs me he can never make a good job of the coat.*
>
> *I should like a suit of the enclosed [sample of material] but I do not dare order it & I have confess I have lost confidence.*

The Cundey Grave, Highgate Cemetery. Cundey's Corner has become a well-known landmark on the much trodden path to Karl Marx's grave (who was unlikely to have ever considered becoming a Henry Poole customer).

Not just the living. Poole's also made clothes for the waxwork models at Madame Tussaud's.

Fourth generation. From 1883 to 1927 Howard Cundey proved to be an able custodian of his family's business.

It must have been a very tiresome letter to receive at so difficult a time. Given his loss of confidence one might wonder why Trelawny bothered to send the sample, and although Poole's might for once have made a duff set of clothes, it is much more likely that his complaint was because he had put on weight and (like many men) refused to admit it.

Nevertheless, the business began slowly to pull around, and notable new customers continued to arrive: the Crown Prince of Austria, Prince Constantin Radziwill, the Prince of Bulgaria, the Maharajah of Mysore, Madame Tussaud's waxwork museum. But apart from knowing she had made an important contribution to the company's finances, Mary Ann saw little benefit: she was the next to die, on 18 December 1879, and although she was sixty-seven there cannot be much doubt that her death too was hastened by the unfamiliar stresses Henry left.

Samuel Cundey's second son Joseph followed less than three years later on 20 June 1882, aged twenty-two. Samuel had realized his son was about to die: exactly one week earlier he bought the Cundey family grave in Highgate Cemetery East, across the road from the Poole grave in the western side. So little is known about Joseph that his death cannot be seen definitely as another result of Henry's legacy, but the additional pain and shock must have contributed to Samuel's own death just eighteen months later at the age of sixty, on 19 December 1883.

His body was interred by his surviving son Howard on Christmas Eve 1883. What a dismal Christmas that must have been. The deaths of Joseph and Samuel, son and father, strangely echoed the deaths of the James Pooles, junior and senior, that had made Henry Poole head of the firm in 1846. Now all the Pooles had gone, the flamboyant Henry, his widow Emma and his spinster sister Mary Ann. Cousin Samuel Cundey had gone too, leaving his half-share in the business to his widow Eliza. Their son Howard, who was only twenty-six, became its new manager and took on his responsibilities with Eliza's stalwart support; but a heavy price had been paid.

CHAPTER *10*

Wampum and War-paint

Compared to Henry Poole's long, complicated and unrealistic Will, Samuel Cundey's was a model of simple clarity. Whereas Henry's covered fourteen pages, Samuel's had one paragraph: he left everything to his wife Eliza. Moreover, when the Will was proved early in 1884, it showed he died very well off: at a time when the average British male manual worker earned about sixty-one pounds a year, Eliza inherited an estate worth nearly £61,000, or about £3.5 million in modern values.

After the financial and emotional traumas of the previous few years, Howard was the ideal new manager for the business. He later attributed his business success to his early education at a private school in Guildford, outside London. Thereafter he 'practically had to begin at the bottom and work up again', because for some reason he was sent to school in Germany for two years, even though at first he spoke no German. Then followed a long holiday, and at last, aged eighteen, he entered the business in 1875: his first experience there was the very busy time occasioned by preparations for the Prince of Wales' visit to India.

Howard admitted that unlike any of the three previous heads of the firm, 'he could not call himself a practical tailor': his training in that direction had been only for a couple of hours a day in the first few months, and as his father's health began to break in the time after Henry's death, he started to take greater responsibility, preparing for the role to come.

Charles Bentley Bingley, Henry's trustee, died in 1887 and Sir Reginald Hanson – Bingley's son-in-law and a former Lord Mayor of London and Master of the Merchant Taylors' Company – took over the role. Bingley had done what he could to help get the firm back on an even financial footing: for example, the ledgers include the details of an American client (ironically another tailor) called H.J. Burton Junior. His account with Poole's was long overdue, and was terminated in Bingley's hand-writing: 'No more orders to be accepted. CBB.' Working closely with Howard on the company's financial control, Sir Reginald Hanson soon showed that the days of interminable credit for clients really had gone. 'Wampum and war-paint', a colloquial phrase of the time, was an appropriate description of this stage in Poole's development, for two reasons – firstly because it meant to be dressed in one's finest clothes. Wampum beads of glass or shell are made by Native

Sir Reginald Hanson became Poole's Trustee in 1887 and ensured the continuing financial recovery of the company.

75

Americans, and the image led to the firm being actually named in the Oxford English Dictionary with a quote from a novel of 1890: 'he arrayed himself in the wampum and war-paint proper for such engagements, as manufactured by Mr Poole of Savile Row.' And secondly, Howard and Hanson were on the war-path against debtors.

'The blow has fallen', said the satirical *Society Times*. 'Poole has struck!' First victim was Evander Berry Wall, King of the Dudes, who in September 1888 received a new kind of suit – not more clothes, but a lawsuit for settlement of $250 of unpaid bills. He was not the only one to face this startling new approach to business, and with feeble puns *Society Times* looked back to the former habits of 'that famous firm of Poole & Co, who by shear genius and the natural demands of mankind for a covering for its legs, have become immortal', without any 'unseamly aggressions' on their clients. But 'Hanson the merciless' was of a different cloth,

> *a person imbued with the firm principles of modern radicalism – that debts are made to be paid. And so, from London to Lucknow a cloud of gloom and terror spreads like a vast, black broadcloth suit of woe. At the announcement that Poole & Co expect their bills to be paid, the cheeks of strong men blanch, and the knees of weak men wobble.*

So far as the public was concerned, however, the big issue of the day in the tailoring world was not debts but sweated labour. The word 'sweater' is a small example of how language changes with time. In labour terms, it actually originates in tailoring and is far older than most people would imagine: its first recorded use in written English was in 1529, when it simply meant a tailor who worked overtime at home. But beginning in the middle 1830s, the practice arose whereby middlemen would take materials from the tailoring firm's cutters and farm out the sewing work, and by 1850 'sweater' had acquired a new and more sinister meaning – 'someone who exacts hard work at very low wages.' The sweater was no longer the person doing the work, but the person who made others sweat, forcing the work to be done at the cheapest possible rate, and pocketing the difference between the amount paid to the workers and the amount charged to the cutters. The difference could be considerable: one sweater allegedly paid only one shilling and threepence (8p) for every five shillings and sixpence (38p) he charged.

Sweating offended the Victorians' gradually awakening social conscience, not because of the subcontracting but because of the generally appalling work conditions, the grotesque level of exploitation (only one step up from slavery) and the belief that sweating encouraged immorality and drunkenness. No doubt it did: the workers needed some kind of outlet. However, in 1888 the House of Lords opened a series of investigative committee hearings. Evidence accumulated of people working seventeen or eighteen hours a day at starvation wages, in unventilated rooms without sanitation and filled with disease. The mounting scandal promised to become a crisis for many tailors, and Poole's wrote an indignant letter to the *Pall Mall Gazette*:

> *In your issue of Saturday last you mention the name of this firm in an article headed 'The Peers and the Sweaters'. As we employ no 'sweaters' and our name has not been mentioned in the inquiries now proceeding, we must request you at once to amend your statement, which is quite unjustifiable.*

The magazine's editor responded:

> *Messrs Poole and Co have been misinformed. Their name **was** mentioned to the Lords Committee on Friday, but in a favourable sense – as an instance of a firm which did not employ 'sweaters.'*

That could have been that, and Poole's could have basked smugly while other tailors faced humiliation in the press; but then it emerged that unknown to Howard Cundey, Poole's had been employing at least one sweater, an Italian rascal called Vantini, 'a person who lived on the labour of others'. He 'did no work. All he did was to walk about and boss the girls in his employ', and one witness said that Vantini's annual takings from Poole's were at least £1,200, while another declared they could not be less than £2,000. Next to this allegation, in the margin of the published article held in the company archives, there is a single handwritten word: *Bosh!*

Bosh or not, Howard quickly got rid of Vantini. One witness hinted that Vantini simply carried on working under a different name, and another that Howard faced a moral dilemma: finding that 'it would be cruel to withdraw all the work', he was said to have allowed some sweating to continue. But no one confirmed these hints, and Poole's gained credit for its decisiveness: 'If all the other great firms mentioned would do the same, great assistance would be given in solving the problem of the sweating system.'

Paving the way towards new legislation, the Lords' condemnation of sweating strengthened the workers' self-confidence and led in 1891 to a new tailoring strike, the first for a quarter of a century. The workers put forward a new draft log of rates of pay, and in replying to it, Howard took the lead on behalf of the master tailors. As *Men's Wear* said, this brought him 'right to the front' of the trade, and *The Tailor and Cutter* was enthusiastic, describing the first meeting of the masters' general committee as

> *excellently conducted from first to last. Mr Cundey made a first-rate chairman. Not only because of his representing the chief trade in the West End, but by his bearing, manner, and business capacity, he imparted dignity to the proceedings. Mr Cundey, who does not appear to have much turned thirty [he was actually*

thirty-three], is a fine specimen of a West End gentleman, has a light moustache and a fine head of jet-black hair. Though he said it was the first time he had presided over a public meeting, he is clearly well fitted to take a leading part in public affairs.

Given his comparative youth, this was a remarkable tribute both to Howard's own powers of leadership and the respect given to the recovering firm. No less importantly, he projected a mood of conciliation, and when some of the masters demurred a little later, he challenged them in dramatic fashion. From the general committee meeting, sub-committees under his chairmanship had been formed with the understanding that their conclusions would be accepted by the next general meeting. However,

it was not until the termination of the negotiations that the sub-committees discovered, to their astonishment, that their reference of the revised log to the general committee was anything beyond what they intended it to be – a matter of formal courtesy. Then there was a 'breeze'... This brought up Mr Cundey, who invited or rather demanded a vote of censure if there was any feeling of dissatisfaction with the sub-committees' action; but the challenge was not taken up.

Howard had his way, the Conciliation Committee was given full powers to settle the dispute, and while workers called stridently for 'The Log, the whole Log, and nothing but the Log', he sat again with their leaders discussing every item. The result, in 'a scene of great excitement, the men cheering for the union', was the new Universal Time Log, still the nominal basis of payment today.

Noting that 'the expedition with which it has been accomplished is something which even the most sanguine would not have dared to hope, when the masters were first approached', the workers' view was that the masters 'took their beating like gentlemen'. If so, then Howard was the leading gentleman. The workers saw him as fair and approachable; the masters accepted his authority as being not just on inheritance but on character and merit; and this episode, more than any other, set the seal on his personal prestige and the renewed prestige of Henry Poole & Co in leadership of the Row.

Having said that, it is interesting to see the conditions in which his men worked. In 1892 one enterprising reporter from the *London Art Fashion Journal* decided to try and 'place before the trade some ideas concerning the arrangement of the better class of workshops'. By then Poole's King Street workshops, victims of the disastrous fire in 1870, had been rebuilt. The reporter was not allowed to see around, so instead he interviewed a former Poole workman 'who recently left on his own account' – in other words, not one with a particular axe to grind against the company. To avoid accusations of cheque-book journalism, the reporter emphasized that 'no bribe was given or promised neither before nor since this information was given', but he left us a unique glimpse into working conditions within the firm.

The King Street workrooms were spread over three floors, of which the topmost was considered the healthiest: unlike the others it had no coke-burning stove and there were ventilators in the roof. Smoothing irons were distributed somewhat randomly: if one was needed on the top floor, you went down and down until you found one. Apart from the premises in Savile Row itself and in Clifford Street, where the livery-makers worked, the King Street premises overall employed about seventy journeymen and regulars, of whom up to twenty-four worked in the top room, seated on the floor, starting at 6 a.m. and going through until 7 p.m., 'except in the summer time, when we often worked until it was dark.' There was generally a plentiful supply of garments to work on; two porters or 'trotters' swept out the rooms in turns; a timekeeper clocked work in and out, and there was a 'valet' – 'a sort of general messenger for the men. He cleaned our boots, went any message, or fetched the beer' at 10 a.m., 1 p.m. and 5 p.m. 'But I'm tee-total,' said the interviewee, 'and it didn't affect me.'

Poole's Workshop No 2, King Street. Rebuilt in 1870 after a fire, it was considered by one employee '...a splendid shop for money, if you can turn out the work.'

'Now,' asked the reporter, 'what about the sanitary arrangements?' These were 'evidently a subject my informant did not care to touch on'. Not surprisingly: there was no changing-room for privacy and no basin for washing but only a sink in which tools were cleaned, while for bodily functions there were several urinal troughs and a three-seat lavatory without doors – 'not', as the worker said, 'conducive to modesty or decency', and anyone coming in could see who occupied the various places. Nevertheless he liked the workshops: they 'would compare favourably with any others he had seen,' and he added, perhaps most importantly, 'I must say it's a splendid shop for money, if you can turn out the work.'

Meanwhile over in the single-storey Clifford Street workshops, a system of mirrors enabled curious customers to watch the livery tailors at work without being seen themselves; but the main showrooms in Savile Row were a much greater focus of public interest.

Everyone who visited Poole's Savile Row premises agreed they were a knock-out, not least because the interior contrasted so much with the exterior. Today many people would say the building's Italianate façade was very attractive (certainly more so than the modern building which has replaced it), but in those days it was viewed as lacking 'that imposing aspect that many of the buildings occupied by trades of far less importance have'. However, from the moment of being ushered inside by a uniformed commissionaire, it was quite another question: the rich carpeting, the stacked bales of beautiful cloth, the mirrors, bronze ornaments and fitting rooms ('miniature palaces'), the displayed swords, cocked hats and ceremonial outfits, the lectern with *The Times*, the counting house arranged like a bank, the jockey's weighing scales, the leather armchairs and frosted glass roof-lights, the open fires in winter – everything conveyed discreet opulence, effortless elegance, with the highest distinctions the least showily displayed.

It was, said one ecstatic commentator, the home of 'tailoring *in excelsis*… a studio – an *atelier* – where tailoring was an art indeed, and where even princes might without loss of dignity be seen in a forward baste' (a half-finished garment loosely stitched together); and another reporter declared that if competing tailors wished to outnumber Poole's Royal and Imperial Warrants with their own official documents, they would have to frame their County Court summonses.

Presiding over all this, Howard Cundey would probably have been best pleased by comments from one of the frequent articles in *The Tailor and Cutter*:

> *Right through our visit we were made aware of an ESPRIT DE CORPS in all we met. The counting house representatives were proud of their arrangements; the salesmen betrayed consciousness of the excellence of their fittings and premises; the cutters were conscious of the respect the trade gave to their productions, and the same feeling was evident in every department, from the pattern keeper to the packers. And we think it was fully justified…*

Howard (presumably with Sir Reginald Hanson's fiscal approval) maintained Henry Poole's habit of 'illuminations' on royal occasions, although in somewhat modified form because of the expense:

> *About £300 each time. In addition to the cost of erection, and the cost of gas consumed, they have to pay for a large force of extra police whose services are required to keep the public from inconveniencing the residents in Savile-row. Upon a fine night the place is simply crowded when the illumination is up.*

But 'as their display has now become generally known to be one of no ordinary magnitude', it always attracted good publicity:

> *Unpretentious though these buildings are, could our readers have seen them illuminated on the occasion of the recent Royal Marriage, they would have been charmed, for the whole front seemed ablaze with light streaming through jewelled coats of arms and other emblems of an exceedingly rich character, quite in keeping with the high standing and character of this distinguished firm…*

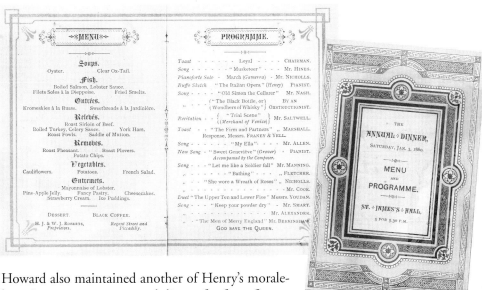

Corporate hospitality. Menu cards from Howard Cundey's annual dinner for senior members of the staff.

Howard also maintained another of Henry's morale-boosting customs, an annual dinner for forty-five or fifty of the firm's senior staff, with songs, recitals and musical entertainments (duly reported on, with yet more good publicity), and he became intimately involved with three trade organizations. One of these, the Association of London Master Tailors (ALMT), formed in May 1891 during the strike that year, was effectively the trades union for London-based masters. Howard proposed the successful election of another prominent tailor, Harry Hill, as its first president; he himself was elected senior vice-president and served in that capacity until Hill's death in 1904, when he was elected president, remaining in that role for sixteen years. Moreover, the ALMT's Conciliation Committee (which Howard had chaired and strongly influenced during the 1891 strike) was one of the first to be recognized by the Board of Trade after the Conciliation Act of 1896, when he was appointed its permanent chairman.

The other two trade organizations were both strongly charitable, working for the benefit of industry members who had fallen on hard times. These were the Journeyman Tailors' Benevolent Institution, known as the TBI, and the Master Tailors' Benevolent Association (MTBA), respectively caring for the 'ordinary sewing tailors' and the leaders of firms. The TBI was founded in 1837 through the generosity of John Stultz, a master tailor nearly as famous in his day as Henry Poole later was in his, and the MTBA was co-founded by Howard in 1887. Bearing in mind that in Britain then there were no Welfare State arrangements, and that these bodies were the sole sources of financial help for needy members of the trade, their contemporary importance can hardly be overstated.

The creation of the MTBA was a direct result of Howard's support of the TBI, and came about after one of the TBI's annual fund-raising dinners. Leaving the event in a hansom cab with a colleague, W. H. Goodall, Howard remarked that there ought really to be a similarly supportive organization for master tailors. Goodall agreed, and in a short time the basis of the MTBA was established with Goodall as its first president and Howard as its honorary treasurer, a post he worked in for thirty years until Goodall's death in 1917. Howard then became president for eight years, and even today the MTBA still provides valuable help to individuals and to other charitable bodies such as The Cottage Homes, a fine provider of care for aged or infirm tailors. As for the TBI, although Howard by his own admission was not a practical sewing tailor, it says much for his concern for them that he was president of the TBI from 1889 until his death in 1927.

John Stultz. Beau Brummell's famous master tailor whose generosity in 1837 helped found the main trade charity – the Tailors' Benevolent Institute.

Howard, in short, very soon demonstrated a strong blend of skilful management and caring involvement with the trade at all levels, and rapidly achieved prominence and a very large measure of goodwill both in his own right and as Henry Poole's inheritor. However, this did not mean he was immune to industrial obstacles, and in 1897 one arose of large dimensions: the United States' Dingley Tariff.

The USA was going through one of its periodic protectionist moods. Building on previous acts, the Dingley Tariff raised import duties to the highest they had ever been – an average of 49%. These included duties on wool and other raw materials of tailoring, as well as silks, woollens and other woven fabrics, which hitherto had been admitted free. For a firm like Poole's there was one seemingly obvious solution to the handicap of this tax: open a store in the United States. A hopeful rumour to that effect went around New York, and was reported in the British *Daily Mail*. Reading it 'with pain surprise… as if forty Dingley tariffs; as if, indeed, any conceivable act of the American legislature could have any effect upon a great historic English institution like Poole's!', one of the newspaper's other reporters hustled off to check facts in Savile Row, muttering to himself, 'Poole's does not have to go to America… It is America that has to come to Poole's…'

On his arrival, 'an inquiry for Mr Poole was received with an astonished stare' (small wonder, since Mr Poole had been dead for twenty-one years) and the reporter was introduced to a manager, who

> *heard the suggestion WITH HORROR. 'No!' he exclaimed, with emotion: 'I give you full authority to contradict that… We', he said with a very capital W, 'would never do anything like that. We have been asked many times to send travellers to America for orders, but, of course, we would not do so. The best people in America come to us, and if they have proper introductions we are happy to receive them.'*

The reporter came away reassured, and only slightly embarrassed that Poole's manager referred to the *Mail* as 'A – ER – HALFPENNY PAPER'.

The problem with the *Mail*'s skittish piece was that it was wrong in almost all respects. It was true that Poole's would not be opening a New York branch, but as the *New York Times* more soberly and more accurately reported, the reasons were 'purely business ones – viz., it would cost too much to import English goods to America, and also the price of labor is higher than in England.' Moreover, Poole's were not at all unwilling to introduce 'travellers' to assist their foreign clients, in America and elsewhere – a habit which still continues, to the satisfaction of all concerned.

As for the question of 'proper introductions', there was indeed a longstanding belief that it was essential for every new customer of Poole's to provide a written introduction – preferably two, as if each customer had to be proposed and seconded. The *Daily Mail* reporter declared that 'When William the Conqueror landed at Hastings the first use he made of his victory was to extort from the defeated nobles a letter of introduction to Poole's', and it was even murmured by others, quite wrongly, that having brought no such letter with him, J. P. Morgan himself had been turned away on his first visit. Howard Cundey, his sons and even his grandson have all had to deny the myth of introductions, but the belief that they are essential is still sometimes heard today. Perhaps it is the kind of thing that people liked to believe, as part of the legend of Henry Poole & Co, and if so, it may have added to the company's mystique; but the *Daily Mail* reporter undoubtedly made up the manager's comment about 'proper introductions'. Poole's has always viewed a brief-case full of cash as a perfectly adequate introduction.

The Dingley Tariff remained in force until 1909 – a problem and a nuisance, but not a disaster. In 1900, another problem appeared: the Boer War in South Africa was gaining momentum, and as *The Star* said, 'The war has spread to Savile Row!' Possibly remembering James Poole's entry into the tailoring profession, Howard had offered a hundred free uniforms to volunteer soldiers. But he had failed to agree rates beforehand with his workers, and, turning on the question of whether or not such garments were covered by the log of 1891, the result was 'the Khaki strike': a walk-out by the men followed by a lock-out by Howard, who was deeply angered at their seeming lack of patriotism and

Lily Langtry.
Beautiful actress and mistress of the Prince of Wales and who became a client in 1885.

Three distinguished 'Cs' from the alphabetical list in Poole's ledgers. 'Buffalo Bill' Cody (above), the Maharajah of Cooch Behar (below) and Winston Churchill (below right).

'expressed himself in language that certainly lacked nothing in forcible directness'. Fortunately, although it lasted nearly two weeks, the affair proved to be a storm in a teacup, and after arbitration it was settled with both sides declaring themselves satisfied – 'So the uniforms for the Volunteers may be made by contented tailors!'

Poole's continued to garner famous new customers, including in 1885 the beautiful actress Lily Langtry, mistress of the Prince of Wales. Whatever sensitive difficulties her fittings might have created for Poole's, one did not exist – the entirely male question of 'dressing'.

The delicate topic of how a gentleman 'dresses' is a staple source of jokes about tailors and among tailors, because unlike a woman, a man cannot wear trousers in the centre of the body; the male genitals must go either to the left or the right. This creates a practical problem of the bespoke tailoring art, because it affects the way the trousers are cut and stitched. Unlike breeches, trousers are designed for concealment rather than display in this particular area, and it is said that when trousers were introduced, some ladies deplored the new fashion: 'You can't tell what a gentleman thinks of you.' For no obvious reason whatsoever, most men 'dress left', an inexplicable phenomenon confirmed by the ninety-five per cent or more of Poole's ledger notes saying 'Dress Left'. But the notes concerning Colonel William Cody – the celebrated 'Buffalo Bill', first measured in 1892 – include 'Dress Right'. Buffalo Bill was unusual in many ways, and when planning his trousers, the discreet note was an important one for his tailors.

Other contemporary notables being newly measured by Poole's included the magnificently attired Maharajah of Cooch Behar (modern Koch Bihar in north-west India), whose photograph in Poole's clothing is in London's Victoria and Albert Museum; the Polish virtuoso pianist Ignace Paderewski, early in his tour of 1891–92 ('square shoulder, full chest' say the ledgers – a good combination for a pianist); the American magnates William Randolph Hearst, Cornelius Vanderbilt II and William H. Vanderbilt; Winston Churchill, who

remained a client until the outbreak of the Second World War; and the fifth Earl of Lonsdale, whose descendants have remained faithful clients ever since. (In 2001, showing that no time of life is wrong for buying, the seventh earl came into 15 Savile Row and announced he had just seen his doctor. 'He says I'll live for another ten years, so I've come to order a new suit.' The earl was seventy-nine.)

No less importantly, two previously disaffected customers returned: the Earl of Rosebery, and in 1902 King Edward VII, the former Prince of Wales, whose jaundiced view of Poole's had so completely turned around that he granted the firm his Warrant as king. Naturally the company letterhead was speedily redesigned, to display the Royal Arms and the unbeatable message BY SPECIAL APPOINTMENT TO HIS MAJESTY THE KING. Lesser Royal and Imperial Warrants ceased to be displayed on Poole's stationery; there were simply too many of them. But they continued to be bestowed from all manner of new and grateful regal customers: new Warrants came from the Crown Prince of Austria, the King of the Hellenes, Prince Christian of Schleswig Holstein, the Duke of Genoa, Grand Duke Frederick of Baden, Prince Emanuel of Savoy, the King of Denmark, Prince Albrecht of Prussia, Maharajah Gaekwar of Baroda, and the Shah of Persia. There was also one from King Umberto I of Italy, who in tailors' jargon would be described as bottle-shaped: the ledgers record his 'long neck and sloping shoulders'.

Thus, though it had taken a long time, by 1903 the firm's fortunes had been solidly rebuilt, and on 2 February that year Howard leased a solid family house at 7 Clifton Place, Paddington. Spread over five floors, the property contained domestic offices (scullery, larder, kitchen, butler's pantry and housekeeper's room) in the basement, a library and dining room on the ground floor, two drawing rooms next above that, and seven bedrooms on the two topmost floors. A large establishment for a bachelor, but Howard – now forty-five – had marriage in mind, and on 15 April 1903 he wed thirty-year-old Mabel Houle, whose father was a partner in the distinguished (though now sadly defunct) jewellers' firm of Houle and Ortner in St. James's Street.

Tailors' Benevolent Institution's almshouses, Haverstock Hill, north London. Howard Cundey seated with the evangelical Miss Angelica Fraser who cared for the morals of West End tailors.

TAILOR'S BENEVOLENT INSTITUTION,
HAVERSTOCK HILL. N.W.

Mabel and Howard had a long happy marriage, producing two sons, Sam and Hugh, and two daughters, Rosamond and Olive. Their wedding presents, described in the press as 'more than ducal', included not only an album and illuminated address but also several different 'magnificent' services of plate variously coming from the MTBA, the firm's permanent staff, the firm's inside and outside workers, the Foreman Tailors' Mutual Association, and 'perhaps most touching of all, an extremely pretty group from the matron and inmates of the

Not just Savile Row.
By 1906 Poole's in
Paris was one of
three European
branches and the one
to last the longest,
closing only after the
German invasion of
France in 1940.

Journeyman Tailors' Asylum at Haverstock Hill.' Everyone admired the taste, workmanship and design of the articles, which while on display were guarded 'as evidence of their intrinsic worth' by a number of detectives; and after the wedding was concluded, the choir aptly sang 'Now thank we all our God'.

Howard's next step, no less daring than marriage, was to open three branches in Europe. The exact dates of the first two have not been recorded, but by 1904 Poole's was established in Paris, initially at 4 rue Glück ('*près de L'Opéra*'), and by 1905 in Vienna at 1 Kärntnerring 13; and on 1 May 1906, perhaps inspired by his two years' education in Germany, Howard's third foreign branch opened in Berlin, at Haus Trabach, Behrenstrasse 47. The latter two were short-lived (the Vienna branch closed on 31 December 1909 and the Berlin one on 30 June 1911) but the Paris branch flourished and in 1911 moved to 10 rue Tronchet, where it traded successfully until the German invasion in 1940.

Alongside these developments lay one other of great significance. Henry Poole had left half his business to his cousin Samuel, Howard's father; one quarter to his executor and trustee Charles Bingley; and one quarter to his step-niece Fanny, wife of his friend Edwin Cutler. Samuel's half-share passed to Howard's mother Eliza, and from 1887 a correspondence (not always friendly) began between the Cutlers and the Cundeys over control of the company, with the Cutlers using the very distant family link as an excuse to seek funds from the Cundeys, and the Cundeys trying unsuccessfully to buy the Cutlers out. However, in 1900 the Cutlers experienced a bankruptcy in the family, and on 17 December 1906 Eliza died, dividing her part of the business between Howard and his sister. The company archives contain a large collection of letters detailing this debate and the various fractions of ownership, but on 2 August 1907 agreement was reached, and with the aid of a loan from Coutts, Howard was able to buy out the other beneficiaries, gaining total control of the business.

A hundred and one years had passed since James and Mary Poole first came to London and began the business. Now, although the Pooles were dead, long live Henry Poole & Co, back in full family ownership. For Howard, with his new foreign branches, his distinguished clientele, his undisputed ownership of a highly respected firm, and (by no means least) his happy marriage to Mabel, all was going very well. But Poole's history had already had at least its fair share of unpleasant surprises; and Howard and Mabel unintentionally left their children a financial legacy which was almost as damaging as that of Henry Poole himself.

CHAPTER 11

The End of Civilization

The archives of Henry Poole & Co are amazing, particularly those for the eight decades from about 1850 to 1930. This is not only because of the company's distinguished list of clients, but also because of the clothes the clients ordered, whether for military, civil or civilian use. Collected in three now fragile volumes (the Old Book, the New Book, and a pattern book of uniform mess waistcoats) the military archive is outstanding – but though they are bound in faded flaking leather covers, 'book' is not really the right word for these colossal tomes. When closed, the Old Book alone is nearly three feet thick from front to back. The New Book, almost as large, seems to have been started not so much for chronological reasons (its dates overlap with those of the Old) but simply because the Old grew so unwieldy. Thankfully, though, the waistcoat pattern book is less awkward, and together the three volumes are said to constitute Britain's (and probably the world's) most extensive contemporary catalogue of period uniforms.

Part of the reason for their extent is the elevated social status of the clientele of Henry Poole & Co. The officers of most British regiments were directed by their respective colonels to a restricted number of regimental tailors, sometimes to just one: for example, the 10th Hussars went to Hawkes & Co, the 11th Hussars to Stohwasser and Winter, and the 1st and 2nd Lifeguards to Hamburger Rogers & Co. But soldiers from a certain level of society could choose their tailor, no matter what their regiment, and many, perhaps most, chose Poole's.

To take just a few chronologically, Major General Lord Chelmsford ordered his patrol jacket from Poole's in 1878. The following year he was officer commanding British troops in the Zulu War, and, given that the jacket was to be worn on service in the field, he was probably wearing it when he defeated the Zulu king Cetewayo, nephew of Shaka, at Ulundi in July 1879. A photograph exists of him in his Poole rig, bearded and very much the professional soldier.

Major General Lord Chelmsford. Although Poole's was not specifically a regimental tailor, many senior ranks came to the company both for uniforms and civilian clothes.

The heights of military elegance. The languid appearance of Royal Horse Guards officer Colonel Frederick Gustavus Burnaby (right) belied his considerable ability as a linguist. He died in 1884 as part of the force attempting to relieve Khartoum. The fifth Earl of Lonsdale (below) resplendent in the uniform of the Cumberland & Westmoreland Yeomanry.

Altogether more languid in appearance is Colonel Frederick Gustavus Burnaby, a considerable linguist and great traveller: his portrait by James Tissot (1836–1902) in the National Portrait Gallery shows him in a Poole's creation of 1881, a Royal Horse Guards stable jacket. He did not live long to enjoy it; he was killed in action in the attempt to relieve Khartoum in 1884.

In 1892 the fifth Earl of Lonsdale bought his uniform for the Westmoreland and Cumberland Yeomanry from Poole's, and in 1905 Poole's was the source of the third Earl of Kilmorey's uniform as Yeomanry ADC to the king. Lonsdale's uniform is particularly striking, with its vast amount of complicated gold braid patterning, and together with preserved examples of gold and silver lace, 'rubbings' of such patterns form a valuable part of the Poole military archive. Rubbings were done by laying a piece of paper over the design and rubbing it with a very soft pencil or stick of wax or pastel. It was a simple method of making an exact full-size record of an intricate design, and even today, should anyone choose to replicate those uniforms, it could be done with perfect accuracy from Poole's data.

Other military garments recorded in the Old and New Books include dress overalls, undress overalls, dress and full dress jackets and tunics, frock coats, greatcoats, cloaks and pelisses, and dress and undress trousers and pantaloons. Also detailed is the rather splendid outfit made in 1868 for Sir

Samuel Baker: having spent much of his life exploring Africa he became a senior officer in the Ottoman forces, and for the role he bought from Poole's a blue frock coat embroidered with gold, and a pair of red trousers.

The New Book and other ledgers contain more detail on civil uniforms. In those more formal days it seems every public office had its own distinctive dress, especially for ceremonial occasions, of which there were many. Each office-holder had to have the right attire, so Poole's supplied outfits for a bewildering variety of bureaucrats, administrators and authorized representatives of Court and government. It was another extremely valuable market.

To give some examples of these, the firm measured, cut and made for ambassadors and attachés (both British and foreign), for plenipotentiaries, governors and aides de camp to governors, for high commissioners, commissioners and consuls, and (of course) prime ministers of Britain: the Earl of Rosebery (PM 1894–95) and Herbert Asquith (PM 1908–16) were just two.

Poole's also made uniforms for the knights of various exotic Orders – the Holy Sepulchre, the Teutonic Crusaders, St Gregory the Great, St John of Jerusalem – as well as for the Secret Chamberlain to His Holiness the Pope of Rome. Mantles were created for the knights of British chivalric Orders: the Orders of the Bath, the Garter, the Indian Empire, the Star of India, St Michael and St George, and the Thistle. Coronation robes were crafted for peers, and livery for pages to peers. Other gorgeous official clothes were made for Registrars General, for Lord Lieutenants, for Deputy Lord Lieutenants, for City Lieutenants, for the Admiral of the Coast and the Vice Admiral of the Coast, and for the Lord Warden of the Cinque Ports. The Chief Justice of Bombay had his own distinctive plumage tailored by Poole's, as did the Secretary of State for the Colonies, the Assistant Clerk of the Foreign Office, the Paymaster General, the President of the Board of Trade, the Elder Brothers of Trinity House, and the Commissioner of Woods and Forests. Members of the National Fire Brigade Union also received their best dress from Poole's; so did the Royal Company of Scottish Archers; and even the Clerk to the House of Commons, the great Sir Thomas Erskine May himself, was not too proud to commission his garments from the firm.

The list above could almost stand as a profile of Britain's leading public offices of the time; and because many of the office-holders progressed in their careers from one function to another more elevated one, it is even possible to trace the shapes of some individual professional lives from the same archives. Earl Carrington, for instance, started his public career as a Deputy Lieutenant (the second-ranking

Francis Charles Needham, third Earl of Kilmorey, wearing in 1905 the uniform of a Yeomanry ADC to King Edward VII tailored by Henry Poole.

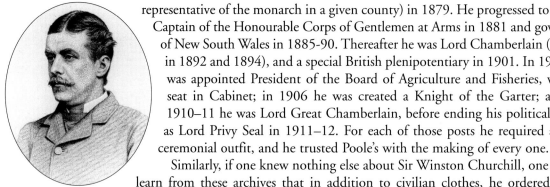

representative of the monarch in a given county) in 1879. He progressed to being Captain of the Honourable Corps of Gentlemen at Arms in 1881 and governor of New South Wales in 1885-90. Thereafter he was Lord Chamberlain (twice, in 1892 and 1894), and a special British plenipotentiary in 1901. In 1905 he was appointed President of the Board of Agriculture and Fisheries, with a seat in Cabinet; in 1906 he was created a Knight of the Garter; and in 1910–11 he was Lord Great Chamberlain, before ending his political work as Lord Privy Seal in 1911–12. For each of those posts he required a new ceremonial outfit, and he trusted Poole's with the making of every one.

Similarly, if one knew nothing else about Sir Winston Churchill, one could learn from these archives that in addition to civilian clothes, he ordered from Poole's his formal apparel as the Under Secretary of State for the Colonies, a Privy Councillor, President of the Board of Trade, Home Secretary, First Lord of the Admiralty, Secretary of State for War, Chancellor of the Exchequer, and an Elder Brother of Trinity House. He was particularly proud of this last uniform, and often wore it as prime minister during the Second World War; by then, though, he was no longer a client. His last orders had been minor – repairing a Trinity House uniform, April 1937, five guineas; renovating a yachting cap, May 1937, seventeen shillings and sixpence, and preserving a minister's uniform, five shillings. But his outstanding bill amounted to nearly £197, and a clerk in the company counting house wrote to him so firmly about the arrears that (like the Prince of Wales before him) he took umbrage and quit; but unlike the prince, he did not return.

The loss of a longstanding customer of many orders and increasing distinction was unfortunate, but produced another more positive result: the then leader of the firm Samuel Cundey (second of that name, known as Sam) decreed that henceforth, all outgoing letters should be vetted by the management before dispatch. They still are.

Sam, the first son of Howard and Mabel Cundey, was born on 28 December 1905. Their second son Hugh, born in 1908, once remarked wistfully, 'If you were to go through the pages of *Burke's Peerage* or the *Almanach de Gotha* [the British and European bibles of aristocratic pedigree and lineage] from 1850 to the end of civilization in 1914, I think we could match you page for page with our old ledgers.' This was almost literally correct, because for at least eighty years Henry Poole & Co were tailors of choice to most of the most publicly influential people in the world. Even so, in the last years before 'the end of the civilization', the decade or so before the First World War, the firm – that is, Howard Cundey, as its sole proprietor and increasingly the spokesman of the trade as a whole – had to cope with the awkward day-to-day realities of business, protecting the firm's assets and good name, and managing the masters' response to yet another tailors' strike.

The Earl Carrington. As holder of an increasing number of important public offices, each of which required its own uniform, he was a continually good customer.

Lord and Deputy Lieutenants *uniforms were re-designed by Henry Poole & Co in 1875.*

From Henry Poole's example, Howard knew that unsecured debts could not be counted as assets, and the question of how far to extend credit was always a ticklish one, especially with aristocrats. For example, Lord William Manners began buying from Poole's in 1892. He was a young man – only eighteen – but of good background, a member of the family of the Duke of Rutland, and though he bought regularly he also paid regularly. But at Cannes in March 1897, aged only twenty-three, he unexpectedly died with an outstanding debt of a hundred pounds. However, Howard had been right to trust him as a customer: his family settled the debt in instalments.

Such was not the case with every noble client: one, the Duke of Manchester, started ordering clothes on 1 March 1895. By 1900 the company recorded 'three petitions on file', and in 1902 the duke went bankrupt, owing his tailor £300, to be paid off at twelve shillings and sixpence (62.5 pence) in the pound. Henry Poole would probably have thought that was quite a good rate, and compared to that given by Scotland's premier marquis, it was: in 1909, when the eleventh Marquis of Huntly became another noble bankrupt, his estate could pay only two shillings (ten pence) in the pound – and even that was spread over many years, with the total still not paid off when Howard died in 1927.

Similarly, His Serene Highness Prince Michel Radziwill, heir presumptive to the Ukrainian dukedom of Olyka and various properties and estates in Prussia, could not pay his bill. In Henry's day the debt (seventy-seven pounds five shillings and sixpence) would have stayed on the books, but in 1903 Howard was having none of it and disturbed His Highness's serenity with a successful legal action, guaranteeing the company first charge on the prince's inheritance when his father eventually died.

Politicians and their coachmen. Not only was Prime Minister The Earl of Rosebery (above) an important client, but also, on this occasion, was his coachman whose impressive livery (top) was made by Henry Poole.

Of course, not every noble client was a bad bet: the Duke of Marlborough's orders run for page after page after page in the ledgers, with items ranging from his robes for the coronation of King Edward VII in 1902 down to a new set of buttons for one of his footmen, and although the accrued sums could easily run into hundreds of pounds, they were always properly paid. Nor did being on the other end of the social scale necessarily mean a client was honest: in 1903 Captain Balfour Macnaghten of the 12th Lancers paid for his purchases with a cheque for six pounds fifteen shillings and sixpence, but the cheque bounced and two shillings were added to his bill for costs. Whether he ever paid is unrecorded.

False advertising was another bugbear. In 1908 Howard learned that two tailors in Eastbourne were advertising themselves as being 'From Poole's, Savile Row'. But one had nothing to do with Poole's at all, and although the other had worked for the company for nearly fourteen years, it had only been as a journeyman; so, deciding that Poole's reputation was being put at some risk, Howard sued them.

In court the defendants offered to alter their advertisements to read 'Latter from Poole's', thereby removing the implication that both men had worked there, and Mr Justice Parker promptly dismissed the case with costs. The *Pall Mall Gazette* enjoyed the episode:

> *To have breathed the atmosphere of Poole's seems to involve a kind of sartorial benediction… legal discussion turned and twisted on the placing of a comma… But as advertisement is the life of trade, and as the case gets more than a column of the "Times", we see no reason why both sides should not be perfectly content.*

Trade journals thought otherwise. In particular, *The Master Tailor and Cutters' Gazette* pointed out that the skills of a journeyman tailor were far less than those of a cutter and that any unsuspecting member of the public would assume the Eastbourne tailors were much more skilled and experienced than was really the case. The problem was that although they had not lied, they had been 'deliberately creating a false impression which is actually as misleading' – yet because no lie had taken place, 'nothing can be done'. The article continued:

> *We can easily imagine a small army of traders "from Poole's", for there is now a real temptation to all and sundry of the employees, past, present, and future, to trade on the great name and reputation which that firm has achieved. While it may be to an extent excusable for any one who has occupied a responsible position to so act, it will be considered monstrous that the present position should be legally authorized. We suggest that a different decision would have been given, and properly so, by a jury of tailors.*

Howard quickly learned a lesson from this, writing into contracts of employment a clause specifying that an employee should 'not at any time thereafter … directly or indirectly use … the words "late of" "formerly" or "from" coupled with Henry Poole & Co, or Henry Poole or Poole's…'

Contracts also included clauses of confidentiality while in the firm's employ or afterwards; of some restriction on subsequent trading (for twelve months after employment, no ex-employee should work in partnership or as a principal within three hundred yards of Poole's premises in the UK or abroad), and of behaviour: an employee should conduct himself 'faithfully and diligently and according to the best of his skill and ability… and do all in his power to promote the interests of the said Firm and shall do no act or thing which is or may be in any way detrimental to the best interests of the Firm.'

All these straightforward clauses were in the contract signed on 18 January 1910 when Howard took on a new Head Cutter; but as he found, it was not possible to enforce harmony.

The new Head Cutter's original name was William Gustavus Brinkmann and his original nationality German: he was first employed by Poole's in 1897, and dropped the second 'n' when he became a naturalized Briton in 1908. His saga of 1910-16 is a sorry one, not least because it ended in yet more litigation. But it is also notable in being, in the whole of Poole's history, the one and only recorded example of really bad relationships within the firm.

Brinkman had an important, genuine strength – he was a very talented tailor, and when he chose to, he produced clothes (particularly uniforms) which Howard admired very much: in 1907 he had selected Brinkman to make Winston Churchill's 'blue super 2nd class full dress uniform dress coat, lined & richly embroidered gold &c,' at a cost of over £110. But the cutter's other qualities were less admirable. He was greedy and much less than truthful. His promotion brought him an annual base salary of a thousand pounds, yet when he came to sign the contract he pretended Howard had offered a thousand guineas, five per cent more. He was also highly argumentative. Worse still, he could easily and plausibly dissemble and shift blame, and as Howard's other employees discovered, he was an exceptionally difficult man to work with when placed in some authority.

Howard knew Brinkman and others had argued in the past, because he had had to arbitrate several such events. However, each time he had decided there was fault on both sides, and his diary and his testimony in court show that even though there were very early signs, for a long time after Brinkman's promotion he was unaware of the tensions building up in the cutting room and other parts of the workshops.

At the time Howard employed upwards of seventy permanent staff and about two hundred sewing tailors inside and outside the workshops. The firm was extremely busy and productive, and had a very high reputation for punctuality and attention to detail. With making new suits, coats, trousers and uniforms, and repairing or altering old ones, about 14,000 garments a year (an average of forty-five items every working day) were despatched to customers. To maintain these standards and meet this demand it was essential for all departments to communicate efficiently both internally and with each other; as Howard said later, 'it would be disastrous if they did not', and he believed he had a good system in place. In many West End tailoring houses, cutters would act as salesmen as well, but not in Henry Poole's: 'It is not my policy. In my business, the salesman takes the order and carries out the commercial part of the transaction while the cutter carries out the manufacturing side of it.'

Until about 1904 inter-departmental communication had been by speaking-tubes, but this had sometimes led to misunderstanding and confusion, so since then all messages had been written down. If garments were brought in for alteration, an

New modes of travel required new types of clothing. The 'Eloop' motoring coat was designed specifically by Poole's in 1904 to protect drivers and their passengers from the rigours of travelling by motor car.

inventory of all items had to be made before they were passed to the workers, and for every order, whether alterations or new garments, the last person with the customer (usually the coat cutter) had to write down the customer's instructions as to date, time and place of delivery, passing this information on slips of paper to the trouser cutters and vest cutters to ensure that all were ready simultaneously and punctually. It was a simple system and should have worked well.

However, problems started as soon as Brinkman became Head Cutter. An immediate hint that all might not be well came when a member of staff reminded Howard that he had not officially informed the cutting-room of Brinkman's new status. Had Brinkman been welcome, an official announcement would hardly have been necessary. Next there began disputes about the accurate and proper transmission of the order slips. Brinkman suggested, and Howard agreed, that the slips should be written in duplicate with carbon paper. Again it was simple and should have worked well, but Brinkman himself routinely ignored the discipline, leaving others to coordinate the readiness of garments and their timely delivery, often by expensive emergency means.

There were many other early warnings. One of Brinkman's unpleasant characteristics was to enhance his personal standing by criticizing others. For instance, when a colleague with the fateful name of MacBeth complained about Brinkman to Howard, Brinkman derided his work, saying no one could make an artist out of him. Howard told poor MacBeth that he 'must regard Brinkman as my deputy', and MacBeth left soon afterwards. Similarly, Brinkman criticized his own predecessor, the elderly Mr Dent ('Coats' in Henry Poole's time) and showed special disfavour to anyone who had worked under Dent. Inside fifteen months of his promotion they had all been 'driven out' by his behaviour, and other sewing tailors of as much as thirty years' standing with the firm found themselves with next to no work while others – noticeably, all foreigners – were given plenty. In March 1912 Brinkman told a Mr Daly, secretary of the Association of Sewing Tailors and Tailoresses, that this was because 'English tailors were no good compared with foreigners.'

Daly had already learned that throughout the trade it was recognized Brinkman used every possible method to make the workers' lives unbearable, and after this initial meeting 'he felt the rumours were quite justified', but Howard knew little of them. His other staff felt they should be able to cope by themselves and attempted to protect him from their disagreeable experiences, such as Brinkman's habitual foul and profane language to the workers – audible, some feared, to customers in the showroom. Moreover, through 1911-13, Howard was being distracted by three further events: a house move, the London tailors' strike of 1912, and his voluntary participation in a High Court libel case between two other tailoring firms.

A house move always takes a fair amount of attention, however much one might be able to delegate, and in 1911 the Cundeys left 7 Clifton Place for 13 Queen's

Dressing gowns (above and opposite). Well tailored bedroom wear was an essential part of a fashionable gentleman's wardrobe.

Gate in South Kensington, a superbly fashionable address. They had barely settled in when the strike of 1912 began. Bernard Weatherill, Speaker of the House of Commons 1984–92 and himself a master tailor, once referred to it as 'the last really decent tailors' strike'. This was true in terms of the numbers of sewing tailors and tailoring firms involved, but in all other respects the strike was a failure. Between thirty and forty thousand men and women ceased work, affecting at least eighty-one firms large and small – such was the scale of the industry in London at the time. The strikers had two objectives: an increase of pay above the log rates negotiated in 1891, and a large restriction on the amount of outworking. But only about five thousand of the strikers were active trade unionists, and this time (led again by Howard Cundey) the master tailors were unsympathetic, because the 1891 log had been peaceably renegotiated in 1909 and outworking was more or less a physical necessity for the trade. As strike parades became politicized, with bands playing France's revolutionary anthem the *Marseillaise* and members of the Anarchist League waving banners and selling literature, the two unions involved fell out with each other, and after five weeks it was over with nothing having been gained.

As to the libel case, its protagonists were Wilkinson and Son, who for many years had done occasional work for Poole's, and the City-based Ede Son and Ravenscroft, makers of academic gowns and chivalric mantles. The problem here was that garments made by Wilkinson and Son in their own right were sent for trimming to Ede Son and Ravenscroft, who upset the former by placing their own maker's stamp in the finished product. Mr Wilkinson's view was that if Wilkinson and Son were happy to make occasionally for Henry Poole & Co and have Poole's stamp in garments which they, Wilkinson's, had actually made, then Ede Son and Ravenscroft should behave likewise. Howard supported this, writing a number of letters to each party, but without eventual success – Mr Wilkinson's last letter on the subject to him was dated 18 February 1913 and concluded: 'I am sorry my news is not good, & I am feeling very sick of everything.'

Because of these long distractions and his staff's protective attitude, it was not until September 1914 that Howard began to accept that with Brinkman, he had a real problem on his hands. War had broken out with Germany in the August, and when his staff refused to accept Brinkman's contribution to a patriotic fund he chastised them for their 'un-English' behaviour. He also defended Brinkman to a customer's wife who complained that her husband's uniforms were being made by a German. But Brinkman's approach to punctual delivery was as indolent as ever, and when Howard discovered that the Duke of Marlborough had come round personally at 8.20 one evening, demanding 'in a rage' to know why his uniforms had not been delivered as promised and swearing never to return to Poole's, he realized things had gone too far.

It was made worse because Brinkman tried to conceal his neglect, which only came to light when John Vince, head of Packing and Forwarding, arrived early at work and overheard him warning the night watchman not to say anything. Vince had already had to make good so often for Brinkman's belated deliveries that the two men were no longer on speaking terms. On this occasion, recognizing its seriousness, he reported the matter to Howard, who wrote an abject apology to the Duke and censured Brinkman severely; yet though deeply dissatisfied, Howard still did not feel he had sufficient grounds for dismissal – 'the trouble he caused me was to some extent counterbalanced by the excellence of his productions... when he really put his back into his work.'

Howard then began to receive anonymous hate mail, which he ignored, but as complaints mounted from staff (at least one was 'afraid to go near Brinkman'), from customers, from the Paris branch and from his travellers to America, he took his Head Cutter to task and received astonishingly arrogant replies to his questions. He also indirectly gained confirmation of something he had long suspected, that his employee was describing himself as a partner in the business; and when Brinkman went on holiday Howard saw such a 'different spirit in the staff and harmony in the workplace' that 'it was brought home to me how necessary it was to get rid of Brinkman'.

The showdown was on 25 August 1915. Brinkman was offered and accepted his commission to date and his salary to the end of the year. He came to collect them at 3 p.m. the following day, and at 4 p.m. Howard received a solicitor's letter requesting Brinkman's reinstatement. Howard replied through his own solicitor; the matter moved on the High Court, running through to the spring of 1916; and the extraordinary conclusion of the saga is to say that Brinkman must have had a very good lawyer, because although he did not get his job back, Howard ended up paying him two thousand pounds plus interest.

By then Howard may well have felt it was worth it to see the back of Brinkman, but it came at a difficult time. Although the firm began as a military tailor's, no war since Napoleonic times has ever been beneficial to Poole's – rather the reverse. From the outbreak of war with Germany in August 1914 trade had been diminishing, and as the conflict continued, more and more of the firm's customers were signed off the accounts as 'Dead'. Although it is a cliché to say that the flower of a whole generation of young British manhood was destroyed in the trenches and the battlefields of the Somme and Flanders, nonetheless it is true, and for Poole's it was an all too painful reality of the day, both in patriotic and commercial terms. The First World War of 1914–18 might not have brought 'the end of civilization' as Hugh Cundey later lamented, but it did herald its transformation, bringing the physical, political and economic erosion, and even destruction, of much of the British and European aristocratic way of life hitherto served by Henry Poole & Co.

CHAPTER 12

Poole Has Spoken

Howard Cundey's diary for 1913 contains a short but surprising note. On 27 June His Excellency the Ambassador of Japan placed an order for a uniform and some 'mufti', or civilian dress. The ambassador and members of his staff had ordered before and had all been personally measured; yet on this occasion he provided a set of other measurements, meaning the customer was new to Poole's but was not going to see the tailors himself. Who could the order be for? 'Presumably', Howard wrote laconically, 'for H.M. Emperor of Japan.'

No other tailor in the world could have penned such a calm, even nonchalant, note. For anyone else it would have been the cause of rejoicing and self-congratulation; for Poole's, it was part of the routine. Nonetheless it was special enough for Howard to place the order in the hands of the man he believed to be best for the job: William Gustavus Brinkman, Head Cutter. This was of course before Brinkman was sacked, and not the brightest idea of Howard's life.

At that very time Brinkman was at his most odious and big-headed. His position and great skill at cutting were bringing him into increased personal contact with customers of the highest distinction: three times – once at Westminster Abbey and twice at Windsor Castle – he had attended the Knights of the Garter, members of England's oldest Order of chivalry, to assist them with their robing, and was about to perform the same service for King George V at Buckingham Palace. Passing the mufti order to another cutter, Mr Simpson, he made the uniform as requested, but he was not in the mood to bother about the details of delivery.

A month went by before the 'very annoyed' ambassador complained that his instructions for delivery had not been followed and the clothes were overdue. It was the eighth time in eight weeks that a delay in delivery was directly traceable to Brinkman's neglect, but he promptly tried to shift the blame onto Mr Simpson. John Vince, head of Packing, wrote derisively in his diary, 'Mr Simpson did not see the Ambassador so was quite unable to take instructions. We had to send Mr Lee to Grosvenor Square to tender a personal apology.'

Gentlemanly behaviour.
This 1907 fashion plate reflects the standard expected of those dressed by Henry Poole.

Royal suits by cable. In 1921 Henry Poole's cutters met the Crown Prince of Japan in Gibraltar on his way to the UK, cabled his measurements back to Savile Row and thus, on arrival, the future Emperor Hirohito was immaculately dressed in western clothes for his first official functions. Below (left to right): the Crown Prince of Japan, the Prince of Wales, the Prince Kan'in, the Duke of Connaught.

Brinkman seemed unable to understand that in business, nothing is more valuable than a good reputation and that his laziness over punctuality was beginning to damage one of the firm's prime assets. Fortunately, of course, he was eventually if expensively shown the door; more fortunately still, no long term damage was done to Poole's name. Indeed, we can only suppose that the emperor (if the order was for him) was favourably impressed by the firm's workmanship, because in April 1921 Poole's was in the papers once again: SUITS BY CABLE – ENGLISH CLOTHES FOR JAPAN'S CROWN PRINCE.

Even if Henry Poole & Co had never done anything else to merit a place in the history books, this achievement would have been enough. The Imperial Household of Japan had existed for over 2,500 years, yet no Crown Prince had ever journeyed outside Japan: their personal safety was too important. But on the evening of 3 March 1921 twenty-year-old Crown Prince Hirohito did just that, travelling in a 16,000-ton battleship, en route for a tour of Britain and continental Europe. His essential purpose was political (the Anglo-Japanese Alliance of 1902 was due for renewal, a matter of considerable interest and import for both those naval nations and many others besides) and his six-month tour was a success both in that context and personally: twenty-five years later in 1946, when he had overseen more dramatic history in Japan than anyone could have foretold, he still remembered this trip as the happiest period of his life.

The part played by Henry Poole & Co in the experience was small but important: the provision of appropriate Western-style clothes, individually made to fit the Crown Prince's slight frame and, by their comfort, to strengthen the young man's necessary sense of self-confidence. 'Carrying plentiful patterns', a company representative travelled out to Gibraltar, met the Crown Prince on arrival and cabled the imperial measurements and choices of clothing to London so that 'a considerable part' of the order (which included civilian and military garments) could be completed before the battleship reached Britain three weeks later. The National Portrait Gallery's collection in London holds a striking photograph of the Crown Prince wearing one of his Poole outfits, the uniform of a major in the Imperial Japanese Army. At the same time Henry Poole & Co fulfilled orders for HH Prince Tadashiga Shimadzu, for Marquis Yoshichika Tokugawa and for Naomichi Watanabe, a member of the Board of Ceremonies of the Imperial Household of Japan; and two years later, in 1923, the company was rewarded with the Imperial Household's Warrant.

It may have been around the time of this encounter with history that a tale got back to Howard which he would later tell with pleasure. One of his young daughters was overheard in a competitive conversation with some friends at school. 'My father is a baronet,' said one. 'My father is a diplomat,' said another. But Howard's daughter 'clinched the matter' by declaring, 'My father is a high-class tailor.'

Having remained single until he was forty-five, Howard came to fatherhood quite late and his children were still young when he was growing comparatively old: when he was sixty-six, his elder son Sam was seventeen, and Howard decided it was time the young man began to learn the trade. Sam was given no choice; Howard simply told him during the Christmas Term of 1922 that he must join the company soon, 'and that', as Sam said in 1974, 'was that. I was not consulted.'

Unable to speak French, Sam was sent to start work on 1 February 1923 in the firm's Paris branch. This was not an unreasoned repeat of Howard's youthful experience, when he, speaking no German, had been sent to Germany; French was the major language of international diplomacy, and so many ambassadors were customers of Poole's that good French was essential for all the senior staff. Howard was not a 'practical tailor' and saw no point in Sam being one: 'It would be a waste of time for you to become skilled in clothing. Much better that you should engage good staff and make sure they are doing their jobs properly, and get to know your customers.' According to Sam's own son Angus, the Paris staff were so embarrassed at having the proprietor's son present that they failed to teach him much, and he spent most of his two years there acting as doorman. Sam himself said wryly, 'Tailoring was not exactly my choice of work', but in later years he came to love it to the extent that it was almost literally his life.

The strain of running the business through the 1914–18 war had damaged Howard's health. In 1920 he had begun to decline noticeably, and his indifferent fitness and the pressure of his other duties compelled him to resign the presidency of the Association of London Master Tailors, something he would never otherwise have willingly done: he had been its president since 1904. He remained closely involved with the Journeyman Tailors' Benevolent Institution, having been its president since 1889, and kept up his active work for the Master Tailors' Benevolent Association (treasurer from 1887 to 1917, and president since then) but in 1925 he resigned that position as well. Sam returned from Paris that year to work in the Savile Row showroom taking orders, and in 1926 members of the MTBA presented Howard with an inscribed silver salver 'as a small token of appreciation of his services'. He had just turned sixty-nine years old, and for the first time in nineteen years, he missed the Association's annual dinner.

Poole's 1935–6 autumn catalogue reflects that the enduring elegance of their clothes is governed by the style of an era rather than passing fashion.

Nevertheless he may still have been well enough to do something he had never done before, because in 1927 he is said to have given a press interview on the aesthetics of male costume. 'Said to have given' rather than 'gave', because this unprecedented act (which may not have taken place at all) is recorded in the company archives only by a French newspaper cutting, and the *Paris-Midi* writer claimed his report was based on information received from French friends living in Brazil. The whole thing was thus couched in improbability from the start. Moreover, central to the article is the word *culotte*, which in male dress terms means short trousers or breeches, and according to the headline, London pronounces in favour of breeches: Poole has spoken.

'This Poole has just spoken to the universe,' wrote the journalist. 'You didn't know, nor did I. But after placing his forefinger on his brow in a sign of profound meditation, the oracle of British elegance has declared, "Masculine fashion for this winter? It will be more and more sporting and untrammelled. We shall wear breeches, abandoning long trousers."'

Expressing 'indignation' that London had taken over *la culotte* ('a French invention'), the article voiced certain worries: one could not dance the Charleston in such clothes, and the legs of most Frenchmen were too short and thin to look any good in them. But there was no way round it: 'Poole having spoken, and behind him all England…the English breeches will be the mirror of the graces and the marvel of the world.'

It was surely written for amusement, and today its main significance is that if a French writer wanted to have a bit of fun about male fashion at the expense of his readers, the magical name of Poole's was the one to conjure with. At the time, however, the manager of Poole's Paris branch assumed the article was serious, and wrote to Savile Row asking whether he should confirm it or not.

It is possible Howard never saw the letter: on 10 July 1927, one week after the article appeared, he died at home in 13 Queen's Gate, South Kensington, aged seventy years and nine days.

Tailoring journals carried very respectful, affectionate and admiring tributes to him, describing him as 'the Paladin of the trade', 'head of the tailoring trade, proprietor of the best known business in the world… a position unquestioned and ungrudged.' But it seems almost a company tradition that some dramatic circumstance attends the death of the principal. There had been the death of James Poole junior, shortly preceding that of his father James; the death of Henry Poole and the revelation of his debts; then the swift series of deaths culminating in that of Samuel Cundey, when Howard was only twenty-six. This time the attendant drama was two-fold: firstly, when Sam took charge of the business he was twenty-one, scarcely more than a boy. The second dramatic circumstance following Howard's death was not immediate, but came just under four years later. His widow Mabel had continued to live in the family home at 13 Queen's Gate, which remained her official address for the rest of her life, but at some early point she too fell badly ill, passing her last days in a nursing home in Hindhead, Surrey, and on 24 May 1931 she died. This had a terrible financial effect.

Earlier in this book it was noted that Howard and Mabel unintentionally left their family a financial legacy almost as dire as Henry Poole's had been. Howard had adopted his father Samuel's one-paragraph Will as a model, and left all his property to Mabel. Her Will was only slightly longer, leaving annuities and jewellery to their daughters Rosamond and Olive, other personal chattels as defined by law to the four children in equal shares, and everything else (which included proprietorship of the company) to Sam and his brother Hugh. Sam then was twenty-five and Hugh twenty-three; and following the deaths of both parents in such a short period, they had to cope with double death duties.

In principle the burden of death duties could have been avoided if ownership of the firm had been vested in a trust. But no one had thought of doing that, not least because with Mabel being fifteen years younger than Howard, her death at only fifty-nine could not have been reasonably foretold. Nevertheless, the result was that with duty of seventeen per cent payable on Howard's estate, and then seventeen per cent on Mabel's, in the space of four years over thirty per cent of the original was due in tax. Immediately following the two deaths a total of nearly £10,900 was paid on account, but a balance of over £17,300 remained, and of course it was subject to interest as well.

Henry Poole's show-rooms - Then (top) … Sam and Hugh Cundey in 36–39 Savile Row and shows the amount of cloth once held by Poole's. And now (below) … the inside of number 15, Henry Poole's home since their return to the Row in 1982.

James Poole, Henry Poole, Samuel Cundey and Howard Cundey had all faced the different challenges of their times, but in some ways the inheritance of this generation – the fifth in the family business – was the most difficult so far. To have suffered so young the loss of both parents was bad enough, yet at the same time Sam and Hugh Cundey were expected to take on the direction of the world's most famous tailoring house when neither was properly trained in tailoring, when

only one (Hugh, who had recently qualified as a chartered accountant) had had any businesslike education at all, and when both were landed with an unintended, unanticipated but considerable weight of taxes due.

They may well have been tempted to capitalize on the reputation of Henry Poole & Co – to sell up, pay the large remaining death duties, and do something different and simpler with their lives rather than carrying on. But they did not do so. Why not is another unanswerable question, because they left no written record of their private thoughts or shared conversations; yet for whatever reason – whether family pride, youthful optimism or a sense of responsibility towards the firm's employees – they chose to continue the management of the business.

The deaths of their parents had already brought them the sympathy of older heads of other Savile Row firms. By choosing to continue, they also earned the admiration of the heads and workers, men and women who were happy to acknowledge the Row's traditional leadership and to see it being maintained. And in carrying out their choice they were helped to a large degree by the experienced Joseph Mead. Mead had been Howard's sales manager and remained in that position under Sam, but he did more than manage sales; he enhanced the brothers' business knowledge and guided their introduction to practical tailoring, and from this as well as their joint ownership of the firm, by the time Sam married on 2 November 1934, they were able to describe themselves properly as 'master tailors'.

An example of the trade's moral support came exactly a fortnight after Sam's wedding, at the ninety-seventh anniversary dinner of the Journeyman Tailors' Benevolent Institution. This 'exceedingly enjoyable function' was 'pleasingly presided over by Mr S. H. H. Cundey, the son of the late Mr Howard Cundey', and although Sam described himself as very nervous, others present saw him as 'a shining example to the younger generation'. Hugh meanwhile showed another form of leadership by winning the London Woollen Merchants' Silver Challenge Bowl, top prize of the Merchant Tailors' Golfing Society, two years running: 'excellent rounds', purred *The Tailor and Cutter* after the second win.

Yet Henry Poole & Co was not a charitable beneficiary but a privately owned competitive business, and its latest financial problem, the outstanding balance of the double death duties, could not be solved around dinner tables or on the golf course. On 10 July 1935 the solution chosen by Sam and Hugh was to mortgage their inherited properties to the Chartered Bank of India, Australia and China. As with so many things in life, it seemed like a good idea at the time, yet it led eventually to the most painful experience of their lives: the firm's departure from Savile Row.

But that was still a long way off, and like his forebears, Sam as older brother and leader of the firm was happy to receive new distinguished clients, such as the manufacturing chemist and great patron of science Sir Henry Wellcome, creator of the Wellcome Foundation. The connection with Japan had continued to grow: in 1924, shortly after receiving the Imperial Household's Warrant, Henry Poole & Co had taken its first order from Kenzo Tamura, managing director of the Tamura Trading Company in Kobe, and in 1930 from HRH Prince Takamatsu, brother of Hirohito, the former Crown Prince who was now Emperor of Japan. The prince's first order was placed in the firm's Paris branch in June 1930, with more orders placed the following month in Savile Row while he was staying at Claridge's, the hotel founded by another Poole's client. Shigeru Yoshida, who after the Second World War was Japan's powerfully reforming prime minister, began ordering while he was ambassador to Italy in the early 1930s and continued to do so as ambassador to Britain in the later part of the decade. In July 1934 the first order came from Mr K. Sumitomo of the Sumitomo Bank, and in 1936 the seeds of a new commercial connection were sown when a Japanese student, Suzusaburo Ito, was enrolled at Cambridge University. Few undergraduates then or now could even think of commissioning Savile Row garments, but he could: his father was chairman of Matsuzakaya, Japan's oldest retail business. And a generation later, when he was chairman of Matsuzakaya himself, it was he who proposed the historic link between the companies.

Prime Minister Yoshida of Japan first became a Henry Poole client while an ambassador in Europe in the 1930s and remained so after he achieved political eminence well into the 1950s.

A total contrast to that long-lasting and stable relationship occurred in 1936, when an order was placed one morning for a gentleman's evening dress. The unusual thing about the order, which made it still talked about in Wall Street nearly twenty years later, was that it had to be delivered by close of business the very same day. The client was King Boris III of Bulgaria, visiting Britain and badly prepared: he would be dining at Buckingham Palace and had not brought a set of tails with him. In a whirlwind of action Poole's measured, cut, stitched and pressed. The king went for a walk in the park, and his clothes were produced on time. Well suited but ill fated (he died, probably by poisoning, while visiting Hitler in 1943), he was able to take his seat in the palace without embarrassment, and he thanked the company with the award of his Royal Warrant. It was one of the last new Warrants the company would receive, partly because since the 1914–18 war there were far fewer people able to grant Warrants, and partly because Poole's already had most of them; but it was welcome nonetheless, if only because it helped make up the set.

The one-day tails. King Boris III of Bulgaria and his Queen walk in the park while waiting for the tailcoat that Henry Poole & Co had to make in a day for that night's dinner at Buckingham Palace.

The following year brought a brief echo of the glory days of Henry Poole himself, when the eighty-year-old sporting grandee the Earl of Lonsdale published his memoirs. 'In 1873,' he wrote,

I went for a drive in Mr Poole's phaeton, which had two of the best horses in London, or anywhere else at that time. I remember those horses well. Each had a white ankle; they were quite a celebrated pair of horses.

They certainly must have been, for the elderly earl to remember them sixty-four years after the event; yet it was so much of another era that it was almost of another world. The later 1930s were difficult for Henry Poole & Co and Savile Row: after the Wall Street Crash of 1929 the economic world-wide Depression struck hard. In 1934, when Sam first chaired the annual dinner of the TBI, the event raised over £1,200; but dinners a decade earlier had typically raised as much as £3,500. Another but smaller problem for master tailors in the 1930s was the introduction of the zip fastener. Helpful for everyone else, for the bespoke tailoring industry this meant a new review of rates of pay; and a further impediment arose in 1938 for the actual as well as the generic Savile Row. A police station was to be built in the Row. It had to have a name, and the original official intention was that it should be called the Savile Row Police Station; but the resident tailors saw this as a potential devaluation of their collective title, and the Cundey brothers successfully led a campaign of opposition. The police station is there and everyone has become used to it; but it is the West End Central Police Station.

It might seem surprising that Sam and Hugh had the time to worry about such things, because this was the period of the Munich Crisis. Austria had been forcibly united with Germany in March; in conference with Hitler and Mussolini, the British and French prime ministers Neville Chamberlain and Edouard Daladier had agreed to the dismemberment of Czechoslovakia; trenches were being dug in Hyde Park. Yet even in a time of high international tension life must continue as best it may, and Poole's could count themselves lucky: the Depression proved too much for at least one other tailoring business, and on 1 January 1939 the hundred-year-old company Hill Brothers gave up the struggle. Its owners Hal, Osmond and Howard Hill sold the firm with stock and good will to Poole's, and while Hill Brothers retained its identity (and Poole's kept on as many as possible of its workers) the brothers Hill left tailoring.

After the Munich Crisis, war with Germany was increasingly seen as inevitable. The crisis did at least teach British people how under-prepared they were, and in the following twelve months, everyone in Henry Poole & Co underwent appropriate training, while much new building-work was done and new roles were allotted. Sam and Hugh would supervise fire-fighting; a staff member who was an experienced superintendent in the voluntary St John's Ambulance Brigade would act as controller of Air-Raid Precautions (ARP). An air-conditioned shelter capable of holding seventy-five people was prepared, protected by sandbags at front and back and supplied with food and tea; gas masks and ARP lanterns were ready for distribution; medical equipment was complete. Haversacks were packed with bandages; blankets for stretchers had been made from cloth remnants, and splints from cloth boards. A large cistern, well sand-bagged, had been installed on the roof for emergency water, the four glass skylights had been protected with wire netting, and fire appliances were set up in various parts of the building, with stirrup pumps and buckets. Last but not least, the company's invaluable paper patterns were given the best possible protection: thousands were laid flat in the basement, compressed, with the windows closed and blankets saturated with soap and water to form an air-lock round the doors. By the end of August 1939, Poole's was ready for war.

Winston Churchill *was a long time client of Henry Poole & Co., who were his tailors until 1937. This ledger page for 1926–1934 shows the variety of his orders — not only for his personal clothes and their repairs but also for the formal garments needed for his many official positions.*

CHAPTER 13

'A timeless and slightly regal splendor'

On 4 June 1940 the mass evacuation at Dunkirk rescued over 338,000 British troops from France. On 10 June German forces penetrated to within thirty-five miles of Paris, the French government moved to Tours, and Italy declared war against Britain and France. Next day the head of Poole's Paris branch at 10 rue Tronchet sent a telegram to Savile Row: MUCH REGRET OBLIGED TO EVACUATE WILL COMMUNICATE LATER JOHNSON. It was not a moment too soon: on 14 June the Germans entered Paris. The rue Tronchet branch never reopened under the name of Henry Poole.

In contrast, its Savile Row headquarters – like the Windmill Theatre – never closed, and compared to other buildings the premises went through the Second World War relatively unhurt. (Later, one of the company's American clients, the elegant author and journalist Lucius Beebe, commented that 'whole generations of dust were not even disturbed by the wartime bombings.') Much of the Savile Row area was bombed to destruction: Gieves in Old Bond Street, Meyer & Mortimer in Conduit Street, Dege, also in Conduit Street, and Jones, Chalk & Dawson in Sackville Street were just some of the tailoring firms blown out of their premises. In the Row itself, the properties of ten consecutive firms were ruined by a single land mine. Sandon at number 8 was also hit, and following two near hits the Palladian number 14 (which after the war became the headquarters of Hardy Amies) was derelict, a 'blasted hulk'. By the end of November 1941, while the activities of Henry Poole & Co continued as best as possible, its buildings at

A remarkable building. Despite surviving the blitz, 36-39 Savile Row, so long home of Henry Poole's business, was redeveloped in 1961.

36, 37, 38 and 39 Savile Row – 'the home', as *The Tailor and Cutter* said, 'of the undisputed aristocracy of the male tailoring trade' – had become the temporary, rented base of nearly a dozen other individual tailors.

But Poole's did not escape completely unscathed. During one attack the premises were struck and set on fire by two incendiary bombs. The fire brigade responded vigorously, ensuring the survival of the buildings, but despite the company's pre-war attempts to make the basement waterproof it was inevitably flooded, and down there the water did as much damage as – if not more than – the flames, especially to the company's ancient ledgers. Those from its earliest days were on the lowest shelves and fared the worst: today they are in extremely delicate condition and can only be handled with great care. Nevertheless, compared to the wholesale annihilation of records suffered by other nearby companies, it is miraculous they survived at all.

Poole's also experienced two inadvertent 'direct hits' of another sort. In 1936, in one of his first acts as king, the uncrowned King Edward VIII abolished the wearing of frock coats at Court; and as part of a drive for economy in the Second World War, his brother and successor King George VI abolished the wearing of Court Dress. (It is interesting to note that in doing so, he was repeating the example of his forebear King Charles II, who, for the very same reason during the Anglo-Dutch War, had abolished extravagant French-style court clothing and replaced it with a more sober waistcoat and long jacket, ancestor of the suit.) So ended the reign, more than a century long, of James Poole's lifetime achievement, and with it a small but prestigious – and sentimentally valuable – market for Henry Poole & Co.

Another important, and temporarily expatriate, Frenchman becomes a Poole customer. Like Prince Louis Napoleon nearly a hundred years before, in 1942 General Charles de Gaulle, leader of the Free French during World War II and post-war President of France, found his way to Henry Poole.

Clothing prices unavoidably increased in wartime: a lounge suit which would have cost fifteen guineas pre-war cost twenty by 1944. General Charles de Gaulle was one of those who had to pay the higher charges: as leader of the Free French he began buying from Poole's in October 1942, his first purchases being a khaki Melton greatcoat at fifteen pounds and a khaki service jacket and trousers at sixteen. He also bought civilian clothes, including in July 1944 a double-breasted suit in blue cashmere for nineteen pounds nineteen shillings and sixpence (had he saved up his wartime rationing coupons, or did he not need them?), and he continued as a client in post-war civilian life – indeed the first time he was seen in a civilian suit after the war, it was in one made by Poole's.

The general was undoubtedly Poole's star 'catch' of the war years, but another prominent one was Junius Spencer Morgan Jr, the son of John Pierpont Morgan Jr ('Jack' Morgan), grandson of John Pierpont Morgan and great-grandson of Junius Spencer Morgan – a fourth-generation client. Like de Gaulle, he signed on as a customer of Poole's in 1942, and with the United States' entry into the war, from that year onward there were orders from an increasing number of Free French and American officers. The latter in particular bought quantities of civilian clothing, finding it not only better but cheaper than anything available at home, and by the end of the war Poole's had an eighteen-month waiting list – a good way to re-enter the days of peace.

But not good enough. Sam and Hugh were still finding it hard to service the debt created by the double death duties on their parents' estates. Having already taken out mortgages to pay off the duties, in October 1945 they completed a step which seemed the best solution: in order to redeem the mortgages and gain a capital sum, they sold the freeholds of 37 and 38 Savile Row and 5 Old Burlington Street, and became tenants there instead.

Apart from the brilliance of his name and reputation, those freeholds were the only items of real value that Henry Poole had left his inheritors. The brilliant name and reputation had been faithfully maintained, but although the sale enabled Sam and Hugh to throw off their debts and receive a modest capital balance, the 'family silver' – its substantial Mayfair real estate – had gone; and in December 1945 they sublet their leasehold property, 3 Old Burlington Street and its Savile Row back half (the workshops and offices at number 39) to a woollen merchant, Jack Hardy. The next step, which took effect on 31 December, was to use their newly acquired capital to form Henry Poole & Co into a proper company.

Surprisingly enough, it never had been hitherto. Despite the '& Co' there had been no legal company structure: everything was privately owned personal property, with Sam and Hugh as equal joint proprietors, just as Henry Poole had been its sole proprietor. But any associated risks and debts were likewise their personal liabilities. In the prevailing economic climate of post-war austerity, while a nearly bankrupt Britain sought to regain some economic strength and while Savile Row faced new competitors who were able to emulate its styles quickly and cheaply, this was too great a hazard; so with their sisters' agreement, the brothers sold their business to the newly formed Henry Poole and Company (Savile Row) Limited.

To all intents and purposes they sold it to themselves, but now their liability was limited, and the new structure gave a clear pecking order of responsibility and remuneration. Sam as managing director and first chairman would be paid £1,000 a year. Joseph Mead, their father's (and subsequently their) sales manager, who had guided them in the early days of their ownership, was brought into the formal structure as manager, on an annual salary of £650, and both he and Sam were required to give their whole time to the company. However, Hugh as a chartered accountant had other work, so although he was made a director and company secretary, he would be paid only £450 a year and would only have to give 'so much of his time and attention as he shall think proper.' (His other work, incidentally, was as

A passion for Frazer Nash cars. Hugh Cundey also worked for Frazer Nash Cars. The company was owned by Poole's customer Lieutenant Colonel Aldington who is seen here winning a Glazier Cup in the 1932 Alpine Trial in the actual car that is now in the possession of Angus Cundey.

company secretary of AFN Ltd, the holding company of Frazer Nash Cars. The Cundey brothers and Lieutenant Colonel H. J. Aldington, owner of AFN and a regular customer in Poole's shop, shared a passion for the chain-driven vehicles and passed this passion on to Sam's son Angus, later persuading him to buy and restore a 1932 model in preference to an MG. In 1994, dressed in specially made 1932-style outfits, he and his great motoring friend Alastair Pugh drove it to France – one of the first vehicles to pass through the Channel Tunnel – and in 2002 Angus was able to buy an original painting of the car being driven by Aldington himself in the 1932 Alpine Trial.)

In 1947 a conference of master tailors, held in Southport near Liverpool, agreed that new ideas were essential if the bespoke tailoring trade was to survive. However, the words 'new ideas' and 'bespoke tailoring' are not always easy bedfellows. The masters created among themselves the pompously-named Men's Fashion Council, hoping it would soon be generally seen as the guide and arbiter of British menswear. This might have worked a little better than it did if Council members had been more in touch with the market they were trying to reach. As it was, a significant demographic change had occurred since the First World War. That war's slaughter had produced in Britain a generation where men were in the minority, with a wide choice of women to woo. The women therefore had to dress noticeably and attractively, while the men could get away with a much plainer appearance. But a generation later after the Second World War, the imbalance of the sexes had been straightened out, and from the late 1940s onward, young men faced greater competition with each other in the search for a spouse. Now they had to dress noticeably too – and they did, but unfortunately for the Row, they did not choose its products. Part of the point of the traditional Savile Row suit was that it was so smart, so well-made, that it was almost unnoticeable. Certainly it conferred dignity upon the wearer and imparted to him an aura of self-confidence, but it did not grab a young woman's attention. Moreover its image was associated with the upper and upper-middle classes, and compared to the ready-made clothes now being churned out by the new mechanized breed of multiple tailors, it was expensive.

Not that young British men ignored Savile Row; instead they adapted its ideas. It was perhaps only to be expected that when the Men's Fashion Council came up with a 'new idea', it was actually a revival of an old one: the New Edwardian Look, characterized by a suit of narrow trousers and slim-waisted jacket with a slight flare and quite tight sleeves, and a long slim-cut single-breasted overcoat embellished with velvet cuffs and collar. While undeniably elegant, this Mayfair Edwardian harked back consciously or unconsciously to a time when Britain led the world. But world leadership and style leadership were passing from Britain to America, and to the astonishment and dismay of Savile Row, young men took the New Edwardian Look, amalgamated it with the 'zoot suit' – emblem of rebellious American youth – and produced their own new look. The Teddy-boy was born, and Savile Row backed off from trying to influence the fashions of the young; better to wait until they were mature enough (and rich enough) to recognize the virtues of its tailoring.

Nevertheless, professionals knew tailoring skill when they saw it, and were happy to reward it. At *The Tailor and Cutter*'s forty-ninth annual competitive exhibition in 1952, a New Edwardian overcoat from Poole's won both the Bartrum Trophy and the 'Dandy Trophy'. The single-breasted Chesterfield coat was beautifully made of dark blue hopsack, with velvet collar and velvet piping to the turned-back cuffs. The Dandy Trophy, a twelve-inch-high gold statuette of the Regency style-master Beau Brummell, was the trade's Oscar and brought with it the accolade of Tailor of the Year.

A photograph exists of Sam Cundey accepting these 1952 awards on behalf of Henry Poole's – an attractive picture, showing him in his prime: he was forty-six years old, tall, dapper, handsome and happy. 'It was a result', said *The Times*, 'that gave much pleasure in showing that craftsmanship still reigns supreme among historic firms and that Savile Row can rise to the occasion when the best is called for.' Another photograph twenty-two years later shows an almost tragic contrast in Sam's appearance. By then, though still dapper, he had been through tuberculosis and the firm had left Savile Row. In 1974 his eyes were full of sadness, his lips were severely turned down, and he was gaunt with strain and illness.

However, by comparison with the 1930s and '40s, the middle 1950s were a prosperous time, and still with high-profile links. Two of the company's continuing customers in Japan, Shigeru Yoshida and Jiru Shirasu,

Sam Cundey accepting the Dandy Trophy. The tailoring trade's equivalent of an Oscar was awarded in 1952 to Henry Poole & Co and brought with it the accolade Tailors of the Year.

were intimately associated with the nation's political reconstruction and economic revival. Yoshida was Japan's first post-war Foreign Minister, then Prime Minister from 1946 to 1954, and as his Secretary in the immediate post-war negotiations, the tall, glamorous Shirasu – educated at Cambridge University and with a great

Jiru Shirasu (above). Cambridge educated and an important figure in Japan's post Second World War reconstruction.

love of English style – was closely and actively involved in the discussions which resulted not least in the Emperor retaining his rank. At the same time new clients included the Kabaka of Buganda and HRH Emir Faisal ibn al-Saud (later king of Saudi Arabia), and in 1953 Hugh Cundey went with the firm's joint head cutter, Edward Mitchell, to Addis Ababa. The Emperor Haile Selassie had requested their presence.

Normally Joseph Mead (who had been there in 1946) would have done this trip, but in the approach to the coronation of HM Queen Elizabeth II he was away on a very successful tour of the United States, taking orders from expatriate Britons and Anglophile Americans. Hugh and Mr Mitchell similarly expected only to take orders: Mitchell had brought his shears, tape measure and basting thread, assuming that he would have to baste up a garment and take it back to London as a key pattern. Instead, though, having visited the palace and checked the emperor's measurements, the two men were asked to make a lounge suit and a field marshal's uniform on the spot.

But, they asked, what about labour? Equipment? Materials? Working facilities? All their worries were disposed of by the emperor's staff. A modern workshop was provided on Churchill Boulevard, the capital's main thoroughfare; good British cloth was acquired and a team of workers selected, including an Italian, an Ethiopian, an Indian and some Armenians. Linings and trimmings were a problem: local products were not very good and foreign ones, subject to heavy tariff, were prohibitively expensive. Another small snag was that the workshop's windows had no blinds, and the tailoring team became a great source of entertainment for interested passers-by: several came in to place their own orders and were disappointed to learn this was not a new permanent branch of Poole's.

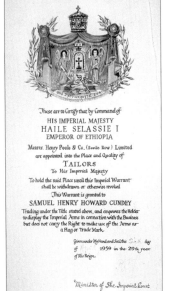

Another Imperial summons for Henry Poole & Co. In 1953 the Emperor Haile Selassie of Ethiopia requested the company's presence in Addis Ababa and another Royal Warrant was awarded in 1959.

Everyone else was thoroughly satisfied. After three weeks the suit and uniform were completed, and Hugh and Mr Mitchell came home with the report – greatly flattering to the Men's Fashion Council – that the emperor had liked Mitchell's New Edwardian suit so much, he had ordered an identical one for himself. Clearly a gentleman of taste; and, continuing to place orders with Poole's, in 1959 he awarded the firm his Imperial Warrant. (On one return visit, Mitchell entered the palace grounds and was confronted by a huge lion. Fortunately for him, it was tame.)

Back in London with his 'enviable holiday tan', Hugh learned that a much more prosaic situation was approaching its end. In November 1950 a large dead elm tree on a plot adjacent to the family grave in Highgate Cemetery East had fallen over, damaging nearby monuments. Because Sam and Hugh had inherited the burial rights of the grave and the adjacent plot from their mother, the cemetery company maintained the tree was the Cundeys' property and that they were liable for the damages; the Cundeys said not, and the cemetery company sued them. At last in May 1953 the case came before the High Court, where Mr Justice McNair found in favour of the Cundeys. The only right they owned, he explained to the court, was the right in perpetuity of burial on the site; they did not actually own the grave or surrounding ground, whereas the cemetery company did. There was no appeal and the cemetery company paid for the damages.

Hugh Cundey who, with his brother Sam, oversaw the safe emergence of their family firm from the immediate post-war depression.

With that irritation out of the way, Sam and Hugh moved into a shining period of their lives. The sharp post-war increase of US economic activity in Britain and Europe brought thousands of American businessmen across the Atlantic. Tempted by the dollar's strength, the numbers of American tourists also burgeoned from 51,000 in 1947 to 230,000 in 1955. Compared to the USA, labour costs in London were (in the view of the *Wall Street Journal*) 'amazingly low', and high-grade British fabrics – tweeds, worsteds, cheviots and others – were also far cheaper: in London a yard of pure cashmere could be bought for $19.10, whereas with freight charges and customs duties, the same material in New York would cost $28.50. When these cost advantages were added into the sum of skill, quality and now twice-yearly sales trips to the United States, the result for Poole's was a rocketing five-fold increase in American sales since the end of the war.

American writers were seduced as much by the concept as by the product. In 1955 the *Wall Street Journal* wrote rapturously about Savile Row in general ('London tailoring owes its reputation to its quietly elegant styling, its extremely wide selection of beautiful fabrics and its moderate prices') and about Poole's in particular: 'an oak-panelled hallway with 31 gold-framed Royal Appointments... a musty showroom that hasn't changed much since Dickens' day... an atmosphere that reeks of a timeless and slightly regal splendor'. Five years on, in February 1960 the American journalist Lucius Beebe wrote a long and equally enthusiastic article sketching the company's past, and concluding that

> *When you have a dinner jacket cut by Poole you are thus skirmishing with history... Savile Row itself is a blend of the old and the new, the former represented by the immutable façade of Poole's...*

Timeless and immutable – what grand words they are; but alas, how wrongly applied. In August 1960, just six months after Beebe's article appeared, the news was out in the London press: the leases of Henry Poole & Co (Savile Row) Limited were about to expire, and would not be renewed. There was no reprieve, and this, the unforeseen consequence of selling the freeholds, meant that the company which had founded the Row must leave the Row; there were no other properties available in that historic street. On Saturday 11 March 1961, as *The Tailor and Cutter* recorded,

> *the doors and shutters were closed on the famous premises for the last time. Inside, the showrooms that are steeped in tradition are now quiet and empty, gone is the bustle that has reigned over them since 1846 and now they stand ready for the heavy-booted demolition gangs to do their worst.*

Leaving the Row in 1961. This newspaper cutting records Poole's departure after 115 years in Savile Row. So began the company's twenty-year exile in nearby Cork Street.

Pooles and the End of an Era

H ENRY Poole & Son, Ltd., have gone from Savile Row. On Saturday, March 11, the doors and shutters were closed on the famous premises for the last time. Inside, the showrooms that are steeped in tradition are now quiet and empty, gone s the bustle that has reigned over them since 1846 and now they stand ready for he heavy booted demolition gangs to do their worst. Sam Cundey (right), managing irector and J. A. Mead, director of this famous firm, are seen in the picture above etting fast the shutters before taking the business into nearby Cork Street.

In this almost unbelievable situation there was one strange irony. Because of the efforts, ambitions and energy of Henry Poole, Savile Row – once the home of eminent doctors and surgeons – had become the world-wide home of top-class tailoring, and the doctors and surgeons had gone to Harley Street. Now, as if it were the revenge of the medicine men, the investment company which owned Henry Poole's property was based in...Harley Street.

The enforced move was 'one of life's tragedies', said Joseph Mead. Sam Cundey similarly restricted his own public comment, saying simply, 'I feel that life will never be the same after we leave here.' But though stoic in front of reporters, his heart was broken; he was never again the man he had been before.

Preparations for the move to nearby

114

10–12 Cork Street were done with the ruthless activity of the bereft. As many as possible of the showroom's historic accoutrements were kept, but many pieces were either thrown away or sold, often for pitifully small amounts. The only significant sums were £285 for a dozen chairs and £110 for gas lamp brackets. Some unneeded liveries went to the clothes retail company Moss Bros for twelve pounds ten shillings, and a set of glass door handles and some fire irons to a Mr Jonas for five pounds. And, energetically baled up by the firm's newest and youngest director, Sam's twenty-four-year-old son Angus, a remarkable quantity of waste paper was sold: nearly three tons' weight in six separate lots, for a total price of eighteen pounds nineteen shillings and ninepence. But why did a tailoring firm have so much waste paper?

Angus Cundey, the very opposite of a philistine or iconoclast, was acting on instructions from his father and uncle. Now head of the firm, he looks back with embarrassed incredulity at his actions of those days, because the papers sold as waste were the accumulated patterns and personal measurements of hundreds upon hundreds, probably thousands, of long-dead customers, including among many others the Emperor and Empress of the French, Wilkie Collins, Charles Dickens, the Morgans, the Vanderbilts, the Prince of Wales – not to mention Lily Langtry and the beautiful courtesan Catherine 'Skittles' Walters.

Before the Second World War all patterns had been hung vertically. In the company's preparations for war they had been laid flat in the basement and pressed together, and Angus finds some consolation in the thought that they may well have been irretrievably damaged by the firemen's flooding of the basement on the night of the incendiary attack. But, recollecting the staggering roll-call of Poole's most distinguished customers, not to mention its less illustrious ones – Mr Jasper Gripper with his frequent modest purchases, Mr R. H. Hughes with his blue tweed dressing gown, the bankrupt Lord George Townshend with his brown check buckram trousers – there is no saying what those patterns would be worth nowadays, with their vast intrinsic interest for biographers, social historians, style historians and fashion students. But when clearing out Savile Row, they were seven pounds a ton for scrap, and away they went.

From the new Cork Street base, Sam seemed unable to resist putting himself through the agony of walking past the end of the Row at lunchtimes and on his journeys to and from work. Each time he passed by, he could see and hear the remorseless progress of 'the heavy-booted demolition gangs' as a crane wielding a giant metal ball smashed through the Prince of Wales's crown and crest, the balustrades and windows, the doors and walls. Did he think back then to the time when an irate customer had arrived on horseback, in hunting dress, and had ridden into the shop? It was a good old story which he had told the press when the leases were running out. As reported in the *News Chronicle*, the customer, General Owen Williams, *rode the horse through the main entrance, along the passage to the fitting room and yelled: 'Look at these damned breeches! They don't fit!'*

Said Mr Cundey, as though it were yesterday: 'We managed to soothe him.' Actually it happened nearly a century ago.

It had been Henry Poole himself who had deeply impressed his staff by taking the horse's bridle, leading it smartly out of the shop and calming the angry general. 'That was the Chief all over', a biographer wrote. 'Prompt. Authoritative.' Not so Sam, at least in his own mind: while the 'immutable façade' of Poole's was destroyed piece by piece, he saw himself as the one who had enabled the destruction.

If he did not recall that story during his miserable walks, did he think of the comment made by his father Howard Cundey in 1927? Howard then had remarked to *The Tailor and Cutter* that 'the business has always been run (to some extent, at any rate) on commercial lines'. To most readers it seemed an amusingly modest statement, but those who knew the background recognized it as a veiled sardonic reference to Henry's profligate management. Sam knew the background, and saw himself as having failed.

There was cause for this unhappy man's self-blame, but it was far from fully justified; he had never had much formal business or management training, the decisions had been shared ones, and the business itself was alive, even if not exactly well. And if he could have looked into the future, he would have seen it was about to become much healthier, because at long last, its formal association with Matsuzakaya was beginning.

Matsuzakaya's initial approach had been in 1959, from the company president Suzusaburo Ito, who as a Cambridge undergraduate had bought his first Henry Poole garments in 1936. Angus Cundey saw that his deeply traditionalist father was 'horrified' by the thought of such a connection; it seemed too extraordinary even to contemplate, let alone do. But Matsuzakaya were not put off, and nor was Sam's brother Hugh, who flew to Japan to continue discussions. The conclusion was delayed by the hiatus of 1960–61 and Poole's need to settle into its Cork Street abode, but in 1964 came a delighted announcement from Matsuzakaya:

There'll always be an England – and we are proud to have a little corner of it. A 'Henry Poole Corner' – the 150-year-old Savile Row establishment of Henry Poole & Co have opened a branch in our renovated New Wing. In charge are Mr Gillhead and Mr Broe, experienced cutters of Henry Poole & Co's London staff. They will personally attend to the cutting and fitting of every garment to assure that workmanship and style shall be in very detail up to Savile Row standards. All material used is from the exclusive woollen mills which have always supplied Henry Poole & Co. Mr Gillhead and Mr Broe look forward to refreshing your acquaintance with the oldest and finest tradition in gentlemen's tailoring. Second floor, New Wing of the Ginza.

'Refreshing your acquaintance' was a nice phrase, because until the opening of that first 'Henry Poole Corner' in the Ginza, only the richest of Japanese had an acquaintance with Poole's: hitherto, simple geography had set a limit to the ability of potential customers in Japan to access 'the oldest and finest tradition in gentlemen's tailoring'. Opening that access was another genuinely historic event in the story not only of Henry Poole & Co, but of all Savile Row tailoring: no other firm had ever undertaken such a bold and radical move. Yet if anyone were to do so, who better than the founders of the Row? Of course Poole's were also the people who, in 1871, had first supplied Japanese clients with Savile Row tailoring; and the Row that he created was soon so highly respected in Japan that 'sabiro' is the Japanese term for a three-piece suit.

Far more than the 'New Edwardian Look', the Matsuzakaya connection was for Poole's the realization of the 'new ideas' sought by the Men's Fashion Council. The innovative association was an immediate success for both parties, and has continued to be so ever since. Setting up patterns and all other technical matters, Henry Poole's cutters Mr Gillhead and Mr Broe were succeeded by Major Charles Walker, who fell so much in love with Japan that he stayed there for the rest of his life.

Back in England, in May 1969 the time came for another champagne celebration, with the appropriate sparkle in the company and the press. 'The "Founders" of Savile Row decide to change their image', said *The Tailor and Cutter*. 'New style for tailor', said *The Daily Telegraph*. 'Gilded tailors', said *The Times*, adding in explanation that

Henry Poole in Japan. Major Charles Walker became the company's representative in their important Japanese market. He so loved Japan that he stayed in the country for the rest of his life and is buried there. In the photograph behind him, a young Angus Cundey shows a Henry Poole suit to its best effect.

> *Today's gilded youths, lost to Savile Row for too long, are returning. They have brought with them their ladies and a less tolerant attitude to traditions of dress and décor. Wisely Poole's realize it, and this week 'reopened' clad in a splendid mantle of green and gold.*

The reason for the media fuss was that, led in large part by Angus Cundey, Henry Poole & Co had become 'the first to have the courage to design themselves into the twentieth century.' To achieve this, the Cundeys had taken on the help of INDEX Consultants, a company formed by Peter Adams of the woollen suppliers (and long-standing Henry Poole suppliers) Wain Shiell on the one hand and Stephen Higginson, editor of *The Ambassador* magazine, on the other. Following their advice, Savile Row's traditional obscured windows of frosted glass were gone;

New premises – new look. Poole's showroom at 10–12 Cork Street was a radical and modern move away from the club-like atmosphere of their previous premises.

instead Poole's Cork Street shop displayed examples of their products in the window for all passers-by to see, 'which the firm considers less intimidating to young prospective clients.' Interior arrangements had also been thoroughly redesigned by David Ransom in order to move deliberately away from the feeling of 'a club or a bank', and the combined effect, said *The Times*, was that

> *The atmosphere is expensive, soothing and elegant, an atmosphere entirely appropriate for a trade which strangely has remained visually reticent...*

Looking back, these seem obvious developments. *The Tailor and Cutter* had recommended them for several years, and Hugh's experience in Addis Ababa had shown unfrosted windows were attractive to potential clients; yet no other traditional Savile Row tailor had dared such a 'brave departure'. But in their own ways and in their own eras, James Poole and his son Henry had been nothing if not brave and daring. They had made Savile Row, and with these strategic moves in 1969 Henry Poole & Co were still the leaders of Savile Row, even in their Cork Street exile. As *The Times* said, 'Others would do well to note it, for today when we buy expensively we expect the package to reflect it.'

CHAPTER *14*

Exile on Cork Street

Angus Cundey was born on 7 June 1937. Whereas his father Sam had been given no choice about joining the family business, Angus was never pressured in that direction at all, and his boyhood dream was to join the Royal Air Force. This lasted well into his teenage years, and it took an outsider – his headmaster at Framlingham College in Suffolk – to open his eyes to another possibility. 'The RAF?', said the mystified teacher. 'But you are heir to the world's greatest firm of tailors. Shouldn't you consider that instead?' Sam was too modest to describe Poole's in such a way, even to his own son, so Angus had never thought about it; tailoring was simply his father's work. However, the teacher's remark sparked his curiosity. He began to ask about the firm and its heritage, and what he learned made him change his mind completely. Abandoning the idea of the RAF, he joined Henry Poole & Co when he was eighteen and in due course rose to be a high flier of a quite different sort: 'the Pontiff of the Row', as the press put it. And this meant the actual as well as the generic Row, because eventually, in 1982, he was able to return Henry Poole & Co to Savile Row itself.

In the middle 1950s Sam was delighted by his son's unexpected decision to become a tailor, and sent him for training in Paris, partly to learn the language and partly to learn the arts of the sewing tailor, something which had been denied to Sam. 'I would advise anyone coming into the trade', Sam said later, 'to learn it right from the bottom, to show the customer you have the experience.' Such experience was sometimes rather painfully acquired, and Angus's first attempt at making a suit was not a success: he inadvertently cut the turn-ups (or cuffs as they are called in the United States) off the trousers.

But mistakes are part of training, and as well as the education in one of the world's great centres of couture, there was a good financial reason for choosing Paris. Although Poole's had not returned there after the war, its premises on the rue Tronchet had continued to operate, sublet as a dress-shop, and in 1952 Sam and Hugh had sold the balance of the property's long lease. Post-war currency restrictions meant they now had a large sum in francs which could not be removed from France, but which could be used for holidays and to fund Angus's expenses. From this he received seven pounds a week, to augment the weekly one pound paid by his employers, Lanvin. Having learned sewing from them, he moved on to the distinguished tailor Paul Portes to learn fitting, and the rue Tronchet funds became vital, because Portes did not pay him at all.

After a year in Paris and two years' National Service, he returned to London in 1958, aged twenty-one. Now came the training in sales. The London to which he returned was the family's traditional London: the 'timeless and immutable' 36–39 Savile Row, headquarters of the apogee of bespoke tailoring, full of the symbols of splendour and distinction accumulated by his forebears. Working as a salesman on the shop floor, he soon became accustomed to and proud of the stately surroundings, the calm and dedicated atmosphere, the quality of the products – in short, the standards created by Poole's and expected by its customers. Whatever the RAF might have lost by his decision, Angus was committed to Henry Poole & Co by choice; and if this was to be his life, he was happy with it.

Swinging '60s and '70s. Poole's contributions to British Fashion Week, San Francisco, in 1971 proved London fashion wasn't just all Carnaby Street.

But it seemed he had barely moved in before everyone had to move out. If he had ever had any notion that joining the family firm meant life would be straightforward, that was exploded by the enforced move to Cork Street in 1961 and by the startling rise of a new world focus of fashion: Carnaby Street. On the other side of Regent Street, Carnaby Street is barely two hundred yards from Savile Row, yet in the 1960s it seemed a world away. Its impact on a whole generation, not just of British youth but of global youth, was so great that forty years later it was still highlighted in maps as one of London's 'Places of Interest', while Savile Row was merely marked as an ordinary street. Nevertheless, although *The Times* once whimsically suggested that Poole's move to Cork Street had been 'possibly to get a bit further away from Carnaby Street', the really noticeable thing over those forty years was that many of the best young designers homed in not on Carnaby Street but on the Row.

Rupert Lycett Green was one of the first, with 'Blades', his shop in Burlington Gardens at the south end of Savile Row. Michael Fish was another, with 'Mr Fish' on Clifford Street; but the most stylish and most influential was the improbably-named House of Nutter, founded (with financial backing from the pop star Cilla

Black and others) by the highly talented designer – formerly a plumber's mate – Tommy Nutter. The shop was one of a small group on the ground level of the multi-storey car park that had replaced Poole's premises, and although renumbered as 35A Savile Row, the House of Nutter actually occupied part of Poole's original site. Sam Cundey was not impressed; he had once interviewed Nutter for a job and had turned the young man down because of his long hair.

However, Angus was impressed, both by the open front of 35A and by Tommy Nutter's designs, and they became great friends. At the very same time as Poole's Cork Street premises were being redesigned to be more open and attractive, the House of Nutter was the first tailoring establishment in Savile Row itself to have clear windows, without frosting or the traditional screen of wire mesh; and by opening on 14 February 1969, technically it beat Poole's by a few weeks in this matter. But there was no particular race on, and much more important – a good omen for the future – was the fact that the founders of the Row and its newest member had separately conceived and carried out the same idea at the same time.

Sponsored by the Scottish woollen mills Reid and Taylor and using 'the oldest and youngest' as a marketing device, they ran successful biennial joint exhibitions of their products, in Vienna, Munich, the eminent Scottish hotel Gleneagles and other places; Princess Margaret attended them all. In the relationship between the two firms, it probably helped that Angus was only six years older than Nutter (who was born in 1943) and did not share the generational prejudice that many Savile Row tailors felt towards the upstart. Nutter's soon numbered among its clients many of the elite of the world of entertainment – to name just a few, Mick Jagger, Bianca Jagger, Elton John, Twiggy, Joan Collins, Barbara Streisand and at least three of the Beatles, who in 1968 had acquired 3 Savile Row as headquarters of their company Apple Corps – and it is hard not to suspect that Nutter's tailoring critics were simply jealous of these valuable high-profile customers.

Tommy Nutter unfortunately died young, in 1992, but looking back at his designs his skill is self-evident. Though manifestly of their time, with wide lapels, flared jackets and padded shoulders, they were remarkably elegant when compared to other contemporary garments – including, it must be said, some of Poole's offerings. At British Week in Vienna in October 1969 and in San Francisco in September 1971, Poole's exhibition displayed some beautiful modernized classics, notably a double-breasted suit of 15/16-ounce worsted with a bold black and white

There's no disguising the quality of a Poole's suit. Even the striking visual impact of the material of this late 1970s suit cannot hide its exquisite cut.

121

A rare and remarkable export order. In 1970 it took twelve of Henry Poole's most skilled craftsmen nearly three months to design and make this uniform for Prince Aserate Kassa, Governor-General of Eritrea, modelled here by Peter Adams – the company's consultant on redeveloping their Cork Street premises.

stripe, and a three-piece country suit in 17/18-ounce Cheviot worsted in green and gold. But the same exhibitions also involved a few outfits that now seem so awful they are almost comical. It was neither the cut, which was exquisite, nor the materials, which as ever were of the highest quality, but the checked and striped patterns – not just bold, but brazen – and the accessories: a white cap on one male model, a shirt fronted with frothy lace on another. Did men ever really wear these and preen themselves with pleasure? Well, yes. They might provoke a shudder now, but we cannot see them as they were seen then, when even the *Financial Times* called them 'quietly modish'; and paradoxically, the fact that they look so dated proves how successful a part of their period they were. It was a very good thing for Savile Row when Poole's showed it could match passing trends; but it also re-emphasizes the fact that the Row's truly enduring attribute is style rather than fashion.

In between those exhibitions, Poole's was given the opportunity to show off some of its very highest traditional skills when an order came from Prince Aserate Kassa, governor-general of Eritrea, for a civil uniform to wear during celebrations marking the fortieth anniversary of the accession of Emperor Haile Selassie. Orders for such uniforms had become increasingly rare since the end of the Second World War, and this specially designed uniform was unique.

'And quite a dash the prince should cut too', the *Daily Mail* remarked. His outfit consisted of a black gaberdine coatee lined with black silk and fully embroidered on the fronts with a gold shola leaf design; short shoulder capes, gold-embroidered with leaves and doves, and with a three-inch gold wire fringe to each; collar and cuffs of green velvet, gold-embroidered with lotus flowers; and skirts edged with gold braid. The buttons, mounted with the Lion of Judah, and the imperial cyphers on the front of the collar were all custom-made of solid nine-carat gold; the trousers bore a wide gold lace stripe displaying the shola leaf motif and edged with green velvet; and the ensemble was completed by a cocked hat with a heavy ostrich feather plume and gold lace ornaments, and a black gaberdine cape with green velvet collar and scarlet silk lining.

Style magazine commented tongue-in-cheek, 'Every home, clearly, should have one.' The only bar was the time and cost: making the uniform had occupied twelve of Poole's most skilled craftsmen for nearly three months, and at a time when a typical Poole's suit cost about forty-five pounds, it cost fifteen hundred. Or rather it should have cost that: but unfortunately for the company, the bill had still not been paid when the Ethiopian revolution occurred three years later, in 1973. The prince was executed, and no payment was ever made. No one in the company knows what became of that extravagant uniform thereafter.

The market liked Poole's combination of classic elegance and its moves to modernity: in 1973 company turnover increased to be nearly fifty per cent up on 1968 – a sluggish year which, perhaps not insignificantly, had been the Row's last 'pre-Nutter' year. It was also at this time that (like his grandfather before him) Angus first acted as president of the nationwide Federation of Merchant Tailors. Founded in 1888, the Federation is generally led by Savile Row, but membership is open to all British master tailors; and as their leader in 1972–73 Angus had to chair the organizing committee of the fifteenth World Congress of Master Tailors.

The World Federation of Master Tailors, formed in Brussels in 1907, had created the Congress in order to provide master tailors with a refreshing and stimulating opportunity to get together in a professional and social conference, hearing expert presentations and exchanging ideas. Running from 26 August to 1 September 1973 at Grosvenor House in Park Lane, the fifteenth Congress was only the second to be hosted in London, and Angus and his committee decided it should be the largest and most ambitious seen so far, with (as *Style* reported) 'a programme of business, fashion and social events which has never before been paralleled in the world of menswear.'

One of their 'quite charming' innovations was to invite the wives of delegates as well, a thoughtful move which resulted in a total attendance of seven hundred and thirty-five people from more than twenty nations.

The social programme was formidable. The ladies were offered trips to Kenwood, Waddesdon, Hampton Court and other places, with times left free for shopping; the ladies and gentlemen together had a sight-seeing tour in and around London, with visits to the Houses of Parliament and Sadler's Wells Opera; there was a musical soirée, a fashion show (where Angus's guest of honour was the Duke of Bedford, one of Poole's most highly regarded customers), and of course a huge banquet and ball at the end of proceedings, when Paul Vauclair, president of the World Federation, presented Angus with a medal. But the Congress was far from just a social junket: daily working sessions were given in English with simultaneous translation into French, German and Italian, with the central themes of 'the modern tailor's concern not only with the source of his material but the problems he may meet in handling new textiles', and 'making him more aware of the pressures of marketing and public taste'.

These were subjects perennially close to Angus's heart, and indeed to the hearts of most bespoke and master tailors. It probably never occurs to people outside the tailoring world that textiles may be a cause of difficulty to a tailor, but they can be, whether in terms of supply, quality or nature. To give a simple example, in Henry

Poole's heyday (that is, before the introduction of central heating) gentlemen's suits for indoor wear were commonly made of 20-ounce fabrics, thick, heavy, warm and comparatively coarse, with little give or suppleness. Poole's still receives occasional orders for 20-ounce outfits, usually from residents of the draughtier type of Scottish castle, but as we have seen, by the 1970s the more typical weight of fabric was already down to 15/16 ounces, and nowadays 13-ounce is usual in Britain and Europe, while in the USA 11-ounce is usual for winter wear and 8-ounce for summer. To accommodate and take advantage of these changes, the master tailor must firstly find suppliers capable of providing steady guaranteed supplies of high quality materials in many varieties (Poole's always carries about four thousand), and then the craftsmen and craftswomen – the cutters, fitters and sewing tailors – must experiment with the materials and evolve their techniques to bring out their very best features.

The lighter the fabric the less it can be manipulated with an iron, and the cutting must be increasingly meticulous. Old paintings and drawings can be deceptive, but photographs and surviving actual examples show that when compared with modern techniques, technical aspects of garments from the nineteenth century and the first decades of the twentieth were quite clumsy, and the best of today's bespoke tailors are probably more versatile and more highly skilled than any of the past.

Time-consuming but essential, these phases inevitably contribute to the seemingly high purchase price of a Savile Row suit. But that needs to be set against its expected lifespan (at least ten and probably twelve years or more, during which time it will not go seriously out of style) and Poole's suits come with after-sales service: whereas the average ready-made three-piece suit uses $2^3/4$ yards of fabric, a bespoke suit from Poole's uses $3^5/8$ yards – more than three-quarters of a yard extra hidden away, to allow for future alterations. (Alterations are done without charge within one year of delivery for UK clients and two years for overseas, but very occasionally customers take the principle of after-sales service to extremes: one loyal and respected client recently returned a suit for enlarging, and expected the work to be done free because he had only worn it a very few times in seventeen years.)

Despite these advantages, the initial price does limit the market, but an old rule of thumb is that the average man is willing to spend the equivalent of his weekly wage on a new suit. 'On that basis,' Angus remarked in 1974, 'so long as there is still the money around, our prices are within the range of many pockets today.' The rule of thumb continues to apply, and its market limitation is not seen as a great drawback in the Row; a greater problem is the limited supply of new young tailors to take the place of those who retire. As long ago as 1888, one of Howard Cundey's initiatives was to establish an annual prize of five guineas 'for proficiency in cutting among the students of the Polytechnic Cutting Class'. *The Tailor and Cutter* was rather disdainful about this, saying,

While we are pleased such a prize has been offered…we cannot help thinking cutting as a profession holds out so many inducements for young men to become proficient in it that prizes as an incentive seem almost unnecessary.

Howard's prize lapsed after a while, and by the middle 1970s the 'inducements' for young men to become cutters were not nearly as obvious as they had been in Howard's day, not least because of what Angus publicly denounced as the trade's 'deplorable' image among the young. But every year there are a few more creative young people who decide to devote themselves to learning the exceptional skills of the bespoke tailor, and in 1974 the Federation of Merchant Tailors instituted a new award: the 'Golden Shears', to be sponsored and presented by the Merchant Taylors' Company to the Bespoke Training Firm of the Year. Based on the results of the relevant City and Guilds craft exams over a three-year training period, the annual award continues to this day, and in 2001 was co-sponsored by Henry Poole & Co. The students receive cash awards from the sponsors, and the winning tailors are able to hold and display the Golden Shears Trophy for twelve proud months, giving solid evidence of their training abilities.

This silk 'smoking' jacket shows that elegance is still a significant factor a hundred years or so after Lord Dupplin first introduced an alternative to white tie and tails as evening wear.

The need for enhanced skills and new blood are constant problems of the trade. From time to time other difficulties surface which have to be faced and overcome once and for all, and the middle 1970s provided two. The first was not specific to Poole's or even the Row, but came when the entire civilized world was affected by the 'first oil shock', the unilateral hike in oil prices occasioned in 1973 by OPEC, the Organization of Petroleum Exporting Countries. Among the collateral effects of this action were appalling inflation in Britain (which peaked at 26%), the devastating erosion of fixed pension values, and, as a means of saving suddenly expensive energy, the imposition of the three-day working week. For Poole's staff this meant a serious rethink of their situation. At the start of 1974 the firm had orders for two hundred suits scheduled for completion by 11 March – straightforward in normal times but impossible under the new regime. The staff got together, talked the matter over, and decided that on the three permitted working days, they would work twelve hours a day, 7 a.m. to 7 p.m., whenever power was available. A grateful Angus was there first thing every morning to make them tea. Calling the staff 'stitch-in-time tailors', the press admiringly reported their decision and cited the forty-one-year-old craftsman coat-maker Derek Goggin, who had started as an apprentice with Poole's when aged fourteen:

We all have good jobs here so it is in our own interests to safeguard our livelihoods. If a firm treats you well you do not mind going out of your way to return the favour. We will go out of our way to help.

Staff loyalty. During his fifty-two years at Poole's Derek Goggin supported the company through bad as well as good times.

Bernard Weatherill MP, former Speaker of the House of Commons and now Lord Weatherill of North-East Croydon, was himself a tailor and tremendously supportive to the cause of Savile Row.

Along with his brother Tommy, Goggin spent his entire working life with Poole's, retiring at the age of sixty-six after fifty-two years' service. In 1974, his shared action with the other staff was a heartening display of loyalty to the family business, and undoubtedly helped it keep going through what would otherwise have been a very tricky time.

The second of these unusual problems also originated abroad. Over the decades Poole's customer base had gradually altered such that only about thirty per cent of its clients were British. Americans made up about forty per cent, with twenty per cent from continental Europe and ten per cent from the rest of the world, and Angus reckoned that the French 'more than any others' appreciated Poole's top quality wools and cashmeres. In 1963 the company had resumed its habit of sending representatives to Paris to show samples, take orders and conduct fittings, at first using a carnet system for the temporary importation of partly-made garments. French bureaucrats changed this system in 1968 for a more complicated one, and the company began to employ a forwarding agent to fill the necessary forms; then early in 1975 Angus received a demand from the head of the French Customs authority for a complete list of the names and addresses of all Poole's customers resident in France.

In all its history of international trading, the company had never been approached by any authority, British or foreign, for information about its clientele, and was not about to start now: 'To divulge names of living customers is entirely against Company policy', Angus told the Customs chief, adding, 'We can nevertheless reveal that our past French clients have included the Emperor Napoleon III and General de Gaulle.' But the problem was a grave one: the Customs chief apparently suspected that French clients were failing to pay import tax on completed garments, and said that if Angus did not supply the details then Poole's suits would not be cleared into France at all. He did not grasp, or would not accept, that confidentiality was and always had been paramount: names of living clients were never revealed without their permission, just as conversations in the fitting room remained completely private – a principle so well established that even affairs of state could be discussed in front of one's tailor in the sure knowledge that no word would leak out. (A remarkable example occurred in a Parisian hotel, when Ambassador Henry Cabot Lodge – a customer of Poole's – conducted part of the Vietnam War peace negotiations during a fitting session.)

Angus, sure of his ground and highly indignant at the unprecedented attempt at intrusion, refused to back down. The impasse continued for five months, steadily climbing the diplomatic ladder. The Commercial Officer at the British Embassy was asked to help. The Member of Parliament Bernard Weatherill (now Lord Weatherill, and himself a master tailor) was hauled in. But the Customs chief was unmoveable.

In April Angus had to send letters to all French-based clients explaining they would have to wait for their fittings; and this proved indirectly to be the key. One dismayed client, international barrister René de Chambrun, took the matter up with another client, Bernard Destremau, who conveniently happened to be the French Secretary of State for Foreign Affairs. Action ensued behind the scenes, and in May Angus received a letter from the office of the Customs chief, giving official assurance that the confidential client list would not be needed after all and the temporary importation of partly-made garments could resume at once. Better still, it could resume on the simple pre-1968 carnet system. 'A tailor sometimes has powerful friends', Angus mused with satisfaction.

His father Sam retired on Christmas Eve 1975, after nearly fifty-three years in the business and just four days short of his seven-tieth birthday. In an interview for *Men's Wear*, Sam meditated on the many changes the trade had seen, but there was one which he did not mention at all, because he did not approve of it. It was indeed a radical development: the introduction in 1974 of ready-to-wear garments into the Henry Poole Corner of the Matsuzakaya stores.

This idea originated in a suggestion to Angus from another company. Poole's contract with Matsuzakaya was exclusive, so he could not oblige the other company; but unlike Sam, he was not averse to the proposal on principle. His uncle Hugh was supportive, so he approached Matsuzakaya direct. This was most timely, because unknown to him, the great Japanese firm was on the brink of opening discussions on that very subject with an Italian tailoring house, and the proposition was warmly welcomed.

Matsuzakaya. Henry Poole's long association with Japan is embodied in their very strong commercial relationship with the Matsuzakaya Group. Each store has a Henry Poole Corner offering bespoke as well as a range of ready-to-wear suits and accessories.

127

The distinctions between various grades of tailoring are worth considering. 'Ready-to-wear' is exactly what it says: there is no personal element in the tailoring, and all garments are made from a 'block pattern'. 'Made to measure' or 'tailor-made' garments are adapted from a block pattern to fit the customer's measurements. But in 'bespoke' tailoring, called custom tailoring in the USA, the pattern is made for the customer – the most limited of limited editions, totally personal and unique to the individual.

Because of this, the concept of a bespoke tailor supplying ready-to-wear might at first seem a contradiction in terms – certainly Sam thought it was – but a vital part of the plan was that there should be no compromise on quality. Poole's would provide styles and designs, carefully adapted to the Japanese figure, for coats, suits, sports jackets and trousers to be made up in Japan and supplied throughout the country under the Poole label, using eighty per cent English cloth. Despite Sam's scepticism, this innovation opened a new chapter of lasting economic success for Henry Poole's business in Japan, and today its ready-to-wear is the best and most expensive in the nation.

But Sam was right about something else. The recession induced by OPEC's price rises was putting great pressure on all Savile Row tailors, and in his retirement interview he forecast that 'there will have to be amalgamations to counteract the heavy overheads we all face'. As separate companies, Gieves and Hawkes had already joined forces in 1974 to become Gieves & Hawkes, and in July 1976 Poole's acquired the business of Squires', a small firm which shared its ideals of craftsmanship and personal service. Squires', established in Old Burlington Street in 1937, had moved twice in its comparatively short life, first to Sackville Street and then to Clifford Street. Eric Squires now took a seat on the Henry Poole board, bringing all his own staff to Poole's premises at 10–12 Cork Street. Similarly, in September 1980, Poole's took over one of its largest and most venerable competitors, Sullivan, Woolley & Co, which moved from Conduit Street to Cork Street and again brought its staff – 'a neat piece of invisible patching', said the *Financial Times*.

Sullivan, Woolley also brought its clients, which meant the expanding Poole list now included one of the most elegant stars of stage and screen, Rex (later Sir Rex) Harrison. In the 1956–58 stage production of George Bernard Shaw's *My Fair Lady*, Sullivan, Woolley made the tweed suit which made Harrison certain to be noticed when he wore it to the races at Royal Ascot; and in 1988, when eighty-year-old 'Sexy Rexy' co-starred with Edward Fox in J.M. Barrie's play *The Admirable Crichton* at the Theatre Royal Haymarket, his formal costumes (a black velvet smoking jacket, and a frock coat, waistcoat and trousers designed by Dierdre Clancy) were made by Poole's.

The Sullivan, Woolley connection also strengthened Poole's position in France and Switzerland, particularly the latter, because Sullivan, Woolley had earlier bought another Savile Row firm, Peacock's, owned by the Swiss master tailor Guggenheim. Among the distinguished customers now served by Poole's were Alfred E. Sarasin of Bank Sarasin, the conductor Paul Sacher, and directors of the pharmaceutical firms Laroche and Ciba-Geigy.

Moving back to the 1970s: in 1978, while Hugh Cundey retired after a brief interlude as 'first gentleman of Savile Row', Angus enjoyed (or endured) a busy year as appeal chairman of the Master Tailors' Benevolent Association, as his father had been. He also began to ponder the possibility of taking the company back into the Row: the Cork Street lease would end in 1982, and although it could be renewed, there were strong commercial reasons for the move, if it could be done. On at least two occasions since leaving the Row it had been brought uncomfortably home to Angus that having left, and with his father's shyness and dislike of publicity, the firm had become almost invisible: some members of the public, and even some fellow tailors, thought it had closed altogether. There were also strong sentimental reasons for a return – the firm's primacy in the history of the Row, and the fact that Sam by then was very ill and seemed to have lost all interest in life. By the summer of 1981 Angus had made up his mind, and on 2 August he visited his father in hospital:

The famous Henry Poole check. This exclusive pattern is registered with Harrison's of Edinburgh.

> *He was lying in bed and couldn't really speak. I said to him, 'Father, I have something to tell you. I've found some suitable premises, and early next year I'm going to take the company back into the Row.' He didn't say anything, but he smiled.*

Three days later, Sam died; then barely three months later Angus's promise came under sudden threat. The economy was still in recession, and although the *New*

Coming home. In 1982 Angus Cundey brought Henry Poole & Co back to 'The Row' and the company took up residence at number 15.

York Times published an article beginning 'Their $1,000 suits last a dozen years. The recession is only a hiccup', actually orders for 1980 were down on 1979, and Poole's accounts for 1980 disclosed a loss of nearly £59,000. Written on 16 November 1981, a letter from Angus began:

> *Towards the end of each year I start to revise the prices of our products and I am always alarmed to see the way in which costs have escalated. This year in particular, our firm's accountants have advised us to study the problem in depth…*

The study revealed something which would cause many nights of sleepless worry: all available figures seemed to show Poole's was insolvent. Called in to assist and advise, the accountants Stoy Hayward confirmed that on the figures as presented, the firm was indeed bankrupt – but then pointed out that the valuation of its stock was badly out of date. Revalued to its proper level, the company was found to be still trading profitably. There had not been a fatal failure, simply a mistake, and on 5 April 1982, after twenty-one years' absence, Henry Poole & Co returned to Savile Row.

CHAPTER 15

Number Fifteen

The company's new home, 15 Savile Row, had rather a chequered past. Originally built in 1732 to the order of the third Earl Burlington, it was leased to its builders William Gray and Richard Fortnam for sixty-two years at an annual rent of fifteen pounds twelve shillings: in post-decimal terminology, £15.60, or the modern equivalent of roughly £1730 a year – a trifling figure now, and a measure of how much London rents have risen.

Gray and Fortnam leased the property on to the Honourable George Berkeley (a younger son of the second Earl of Berkeley) who in 1735 married Henrietta, Countess of Suffolk. He had an unexceptional life and without her, he would probably have been long forgotten as a resident of number 15. But Henrietta was a very unusual woman.

Born the daughter of a baronet in 1681, she first married Charles Howard, heir to the earldom of Suffolk. They lived in Hanover in Germany, and in 1710 she became the chief mistress of George Augustus, son of the Elector of Hanover. In 1714, when the Elector became Britain's King George, the Howards returned to England. George Augustus now became Prince of Wales with his wife Caroline as Princess of Wales, and Henrietta was appointed one of Caroline's 'Ladies of the Bedchamber' while remaining the mistress of George Augustus, – and publicly acknowledged as such after he became King George II in 1727.

At this time Henrietta lived at Marble Hill in Twickenham, and was very popular with the noted poets and wits of the day, including Pope, Swift and the Cork Street resident Dr Arbuthnot: it may well have been he who introduced her to the Savile Row area. When her husband succeeded to the earldom in 1731, she became countess, even though by then they were formally separated. He died in 1733; she retired from court in 1734; and in 1735, keeping her title, she married Berkeley – twelve years her junior – and moved into 15 Savile Row. She long outlived her second husband as well as her first: Berkeley died in 1746, but Henrietta lived until 1767, and retained number 15 until shortly before her death.

The house was then occupied by a series of other aristocrats (though none as colourful as she) until 1849, when it was taken over by James Yearsley – a man who by himself disproved the legend that when the tailors came into the Row, the doctors fled. He was as distinguished a medical man as one could wish: from the start of his London practice in about 1837, he was the capital's first dedicated ear, nose and throat surgeon, and he lived at number 15 until his death in 1869.

The building then became the home of the Savile Club, established in 1871, and a part of the social phenomenon which made this part of London a particularly masculine area at the time. The club remained there until 1883, when it purchased the lease of 107 Piccadilly from Lord Rosebery for £11,000 – the same Rosebery

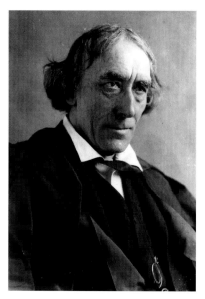

Sir Henry Irving. Famous actor and client of Henry Poole's. Also, coincidentally, a member of the Savile Club which was a one-time occupant of 15 Savile Row.

who in 1875 had complained to Henry Poole himself about that 'monstrous proceeding', the unexpected eighty-pound cost of a velvet dress. In a further coincidence, one of the club's members at the time, the actor Sir Henry Irving, was a very prominent customer of Poole's; today some of his clothes are displayed at the Museum of London, and are among the oldest surviving garments made by the firm.

After the Savile Club left, number 15 stood empty until it was bought by two brothers, George and Alfred Bywaters, with a new and definite idea about its future. They owned and ran a building practice, and they demolished the house (by then over 150 years old), reconstructing it as purpose-built accommodation for tailors. It was the first time such a thing had happened in the Row.

Notice of the intended new building was given in September 1886, and work was completed by the end of 1887. By this operation number 15 acquired the essential form it still retains today – and a very significant revaluation for rating purposes. Whereas the Savile Club had paid £384 and the domestic ratepayers on either side were paying just £334 a year, the Bywaters' annual rates bill was £542.

As fast as possible, they installed their tailor tenants the Stricklands in the specially designed ground floor and basement. A slight veil hangs over this: the Post Office Directory for 1887 lists no one at number 15, but other records show that Strickland & Sons moved in during March of that year, presumably before the rest of the reconstruction was complete. Today they are at number 16, next-door neighbours to Henry Poole & Co. Strickland & Sons were founded in 1780, so their history predates that of Poole's by a full generation, but they did not come to the Row until more than a decade after Henry Poole had died; and it seems appropriate that today the founders of the Row should occupy the first Savile Row building to have been originally designed for tailoring.

The move back into the Row was enormously personally satisfying for Angus Cundey, and was the best thing he could possibly have done for the firm. Desmond Petterson, cutter and company director, posed proudly for the first official photograph outside the new premises, and it was a source of pride for all the staff to be working not just to Savile Row's most exacting standards, as they always had, but actually in the Row itself. It also became much easier to attract new clients: Cork Street is only a few minutes' walk away, but everyone who thinks about buying Savile Row clothing naturally goes to the Row first. So do tourists, and some of them, at first just curious, end up so impressed by the quality of the Row's products that they become customers. 'Though we are hardly an impulse-buying business,' Angus remarked, 'it does help to be in one street everyone knows.'

The years since Poole's return to the Row have been full of activity and incident – too much to detail here or even to list, so in sketching its most recent times we shall focus on the actions which most affected the firm. One which coincided with its return was the launch in Japan of a smart, stylish and quietly authoritative range of Henry Poole accessories: ties, cuff links and other items emblazoned with a new distinctive Henry Poole logo, based on the imperial crest of Napoleon III and designed by Tsunezo Fujinami of the Osaka-based Chikuma Company, who was then Poole's senior Japanese merchandiser and later became manager of all its operations in Japan. Mr Fujinami's classic Poole designs were, and still are, a world-wide success.

At the same time, the actress Joanna Lumley appeared in a Poole's outfit, an event fully in keeping with Henry Poole's clothing of beauties such as Lily Langtry and Catherine 'Skittles' Walters; and if the modern headline was somewhat inelegant ('Cor! Miss Lumley'), the message from the *Sunday Express* City editor was clear:

> *Not every Savile Row suit looks as fantastic as the dining suit worn by Joanna Lumley [but] having studied Miss Lumley's figure and having talked with Angus Cundey, I believe a Savile Row suit could prove an excellent investment. …It would last through the next boom, and the subsequent recession.*

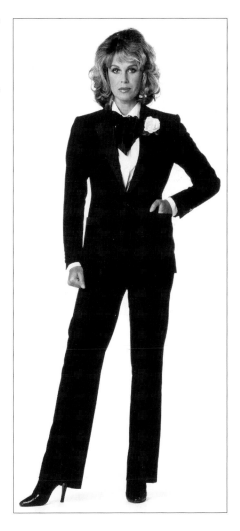

'*Cor! Miss Lumley*'. *After this inelegant headline, a newspaper article went on to confirm the supreme quality, and long-lasting value, of a Henry Poole suit and Joanna Lumley joined the list of beautiful women to be clothed by Poole's.*

The same argument – that a suit from Henry Poole's was cheap at the price – was put forward by Lawrence Minard, a writer on *Forbes* magazine and later an editor of *Forbes Global*. Minard bought his first Poole's suits in 1982 and became good friends with Angus Cundey. He died tragically young in 2001, but in 1996, having worn his first suits regularly for fourteen years, he demonstrated their value. The problem, he said, was that

> *The clothes wear better than the wearer… Over the years the garments have lost some stitches in the lining and developed holes in the trouser pockets, but the fabric hardly aged and the style was timeless. I, on the other hand, am the same person who bought the suits, but there is rather more of me [fourteen pounds, to be precise] and in different places. Were my suits salvageable?*

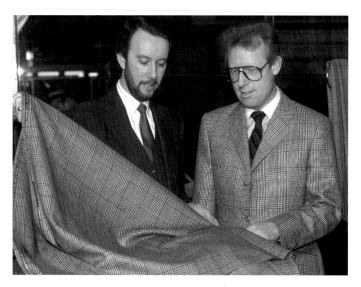

Senior cutter Alan Alexander (left) and director Philip Parker (right) . The quality of the cloth as well that of the cutting is of vital importance to a Henry Poole suit.

They were. During the next of the firm's thrice-yearly visits to the States, Minard arrived for his 'retrofitting' at the suite of Philip Parker (Poole's managing director and one of its cutters) in the New York Intercontinental Hotel. Greeting him with a smile, Parker remarked, 'You're looking rather prosperous, sir', and spent nearly half an hour chalking up the suits and taking new measurements. Minard was reassured to learn that his additional fourteen pounds were not a problem (Poole's can generally refit a customer who has put on as much as twenty pounds), and six months later, he reported enthusiastically on the result. The renovation was so thorough that 'It was like getting two new suits' – but at only about fifteen per cent of the cost.

The thirteenth Duke of Bedford confirmed the durability of Poole's suits. The first of his forebears to become a customer of Poole's was Lord Herbrand Arthur Russell (from 1893, the eleventh duke, and later an eminent zoologist), who started buying from the firm in 1878. Since then numerous members of the family have been consistent customers of Poole's, including the present duke – the fourteenth – and his son the Marquis of Tavistock. In 2002 the thirteenth duke, a highly respected and well-liked client, sent a charming handwritten reply to a letter from Angus. The firm had decided to change hotels for its Paris fittings, and His Grace wrote:

Dear Mr Cundey,

After all these years I think of you every day with gratitude for all the beautiful fine quality suits you made me. I have not bought a new suit for thirty years and the old ones still look as impeccable as ever.

I am now 85 and my memory is not as good as it was, but I should have no problem with the name of your new hotel...

Indeed not: it was the Hotel Bedford.

The celebrated author Patrick O'Brian, creator of the Aubrey/Maturin novels, was, for many years until his death in 2000, another enthusiastic purchaser of Poole's suits, but he once found the firm's accounting system worrying. 'Many thanks for your little bill,' he wrote in 1999,

which I settle with the enclosed cheque. But when you send me your much larger bill (for I must owe you several thousand pounds at present) please tell me about the 'Aged Analysis in Dispute': I have no recollection of disagreeing with any account you have ever sent me.

This was easily explained: the Aged Analysis was a standard term on all statements, but only if there was an asterisk beside it was there a dispute. There was no asterisk on O'Brian's statement, and the writer could return to his work with a clear conscience.

Another writer's cheque which worked its way into Poole's story was from Charles Dickens, made out to 'Mr Poole' on 14 February 1865 in the sum of fifteen pounds. On 3 April 1989 it came up for auction in Manchester. Eager to add this memento to the firm's collection, Angus joined the bidding, but was beaten by a keen collector of Dickens memorabilia. However, a framed copy of the original now hangs on a wall in 15 Savile Row, and next to it hangs another souvenir. The cheque was drawn on Dickens' account with Coutts & Co, who have been Poole's bankers as well since 15 July 1819, and on 15 July 1986 Jack Willson, one of the bank's managers, presented Angus with a handsomely mounted and framed copy of the first page of James Poole's account.

A check of a completely different sort emerged in 1989: the Henry Poole Check (shown on page 129), an exclusive pattern registered with the woollen merchants Harrison's of Edinburgh, established in 1863. The idea came from Harrison's managing director Cameron Buchanan, who also created the subdued but distinctive design; and the design was first used on fabric woven by Reid and Taylor's excellent mill at Langholm in Scotland.

The hallmark of Savile Row is supreme quality in all respects, not least in its fabrics, and despite the village-like atmosphere of the Row there is strong competition between the 'villagers' for the very best fabrics, some of which come from 'Lumb's Golden Bale'. The firm of Joseph Lumb and Sons is another distinguished member of the clothing trade, having been established as spinners in Halifax, Yorkshire, well over a century ago. Every year their buyers visit New South Wales, where a select group of farmers raise Merino sheep of pure blood-line and compete

The same bankers since 1819. In 1986 Coutts & Co presented the directors of Henry Poole & Co with the earliest record of Poole's financial affairs. Left to right – Jack Willson (Coutts), Angus Cundey, Pat Mead, Desmond Petterson, Ken Gambell, Philip Parker, David Mead.

Golden Bale Award.
The ultimate accolade for the combined skills of the wool grower and the cloth weaver.

for Lumb's Gold Medal. The award-winning wool must meet exacting criteria of fineness, length, curl and whiteness, and the resultant 'Golden Bale' of rare and superb fleeces is spun into yarn by Lumb's, who then sell rationed amounts to an equally select group of weavers. Lumb's Gold Medal standards are so high that only about eight pieces of cloth – enough for 150 suit lengths or so – can be made from the bale, and for two successive years Poole's were fortunate enough to obtain some of this very limited supply. In 1987 the London cloth merchants J. & J. Minnis sold the cloth from their share of the wool to Poole's, who in turn sold it exclusively to Matsuzakaya, where using Poole's design and under its stringent supervision, the cloth was transformed into just thirty suits; and in 1988 the exercise was repeated when Harrison's of Edinburgh acquired a precious ninety metres of 11-ounce charcoal-grey worsted with a rope-stripe pattern from the weavers Moxon of Huddersfield.

Though the Savile Row 'villagers' are business competitors, many are personal friends, and sometimes they abandon competition and work willingly together. Two instances of this occurred in the 1980s, one a matter of professional pride and the other a response to an alarming threat.

The first came in 1983, when Angus was for the second time president of the Federation of Merchant Tailors (FMT). Master tailor and Member of Parliament Bernard Weatherill was elected Speaker of the House of Commons, and Robert Bright (the chairman of Wells of Mayfair and the then FMT secretary) proposed that as a gift for Weatherill, FMT members should collectively provide a new Speaker's uniform – a velvet Court Dress of a George IV design, predating James Poole's 1839 design. The need arose because of one of the curious customs of the House, namely that those parts of the uniform which more or less fitted were normally passed on. For Weatherill, the rather unseemly outcome was that he was expected to wear a coat from one former Speaker and a pair of trousers from another.

Supporting Bright's proposal, the FMT commissioned Weatherill's family firm to make the uniform; Wain Shiell tracked down a supply of the increasingly rare pure silk black velvet; Monty Moss of Moss Bros was responsible for the cut steel buttons, in two sizes; and many FMT members subscribed to pay for it all. As *The Tailor and Cutter* said, 'Mr Speaker is now bespoke', and Weatherill was delighted with his new clothing:

> *It's a darn sight more comfortable than the outfit I had before… I am proud of my background and my trade. I believe that nowhere in the world will you find*

better cloth, better design and finer tailoring than in Britain, and I shall wear this superb example of Britain's craftsmanship with enormous pride.

In contrast to this pleasant episode of professional unity, the period's second unifying episode was and remains potentially lethal: the 're-zoning dispute' of 1987. Still unfinished, this may yet destroy not only Savile Row as the hub of British bespoke tailoring, but also other areas where other specialist trades (such as jewellers) have historically congregated.

The background was that since 1963, Savile Row and similar streets had benefited from a law defining the premises of these specialist businesses as light indus-

Suits in the 1990s were quieter and more understated than those of the previous two decades but they still showed off the quality of the cut and cloth of a Henry Poole suit.

trial rather than office units, which meant their rents were very much lower than would otherwise have been the case. For many firms protected rents had been a crucial factor in their commercial survival through the subsequent economic downturns, but economic revival in the later 1980s brought strong outside pressure for a revision of the ruling.

The man with the power of ultimate decision was the abrasive Environment Secretary Nicholas Ridley. As spokesmen for the Row, Angus Cundey and Robert Bright sought and gained an interview with him. It was a sullying experience: chain-smoking throughout, Ridley boasted that he only bought off-the-peg suits from a multiple retailer. He sneered at the apparent slowness and small production of the bespoke industry, questioned why Savile Row could not match Hong Kong prices, and proposed that the industry should relocate its workshops to Hounslow, twelve miles away, to catch 'passing trade' at Heathrow Airport.

The exasperated tailors tried to explain the nature of their trade, emphasizing the value of having a concentration of top-class firms in the city centre, as part of the mix of elite businesses large and small – hotels, restaurants, theatres, hatters, shoemakers, gunsmiths, bookbinders, shirt-makers, jewellers, art galleries – that helped to make central London attractive to high-spending busy visitors. But the notoriously boorish Secretary was impervious to their arguments, and by government order in February 1987 the light industrial category was removed, effectively placing all lease-holding Savile Row tailors (as well as Jermyn Street shirt-makers, Hatton Garden jewellers and so on) on notice that when their leases expired, they would be competing for space with other businesses capable of paying perhaps five times as much.

Within weeks a commodity trader sought to buy Poole's out of its premises. Angus fended this off, but by 1991 the rent on 15 Savile Row had increased by fifty per cent. Some other tailors in the Row were even worse affected: one nearby firm found its workshop rent more than doubled. Three events in the early 1990s provided a stay of execution: firstly a somewhat stagnant real estate market; secondly the development of Docklands, easing pressure on the city centre; and thirdly a stand taken by Westminster City Council, the Row's local zoning authority. Since 1960, when it sanctioned the destruction of Henry Poole's original Italianate premises – an act which would not go unchallenged today – the Council had had a change of heart and now took the position that the special character of the Row should be preserved and tailoring there should be promoted. This resulted in the requirement that developers on the west side of the Row, opposite Poole's, must provide street-level shops and workrooms for tailors at reasonable rates; in return the developers were permitted to build higher than the previous limit.

The dispute is one which, though couched in economic terms, actually reflects a difference of cultural philosophy. On one side are the proponents of a completely free and unregulated market in which the onus of competitive survival is on every individual business. Their arguments seem unchallengeable without invoking some form of protectionism, based, it could be said in this instance, on the artificial support of an exclusive service. On the other side are those who maintain that not everything is equally measurable and that special circumstances sometimes exist which should be allowed to continue. The problem for this side is that the only absolute proof of their argument is to remove those special circumstances and see what happens – by which time it may be too late to correct matters.

'The greatest capitalist who ever lived'. Thomas J. Watson Jnr (left) was described as such by Forbes magazine. From the 1950s he built IBM from a medium-sized business to one of the dozen largest corporations in the world. Both he and his father, Thomas Watson (right), were customers of Henry Poole & Co.

The increasing costs enabled by the Ridley order mean that not only Savile Row but all those clusters of small high-quality businesses which form the economic and cultural heart of London's West End remain under great threat. For each of them, the months preceding a rent review are fraught with tension. Without a change in the law there is no easy solution, and it is still possible that the tailors of Savile Row could either go out of business one after another, or disperse; and in either case, Savile Row tailoring would lose both its magically stylish image and its geographical reality, and therefore its hugely attractive part in London's business patchwork.

But these consequences are unforeseeable, so let us revert to something simpler and pleasanter, namely the most recent past of Henry Poole & Co. In 1987, shortly after their ineffective interview with Ridley, Angus Cundey and Robert Bright each received two personal distinctions: both were made Freemen of the Livery of the Merchant Taylors' Company, and a few days later, Freemen of the City of London.

The Merchant Taylors' is one of the ancient professional guilds of the City of London, with three rankings: Freeman, Liveryman, and member of Court. There was a time when you could not practise as a tailor unless you were a member of the guild in one or other degree, but during the twentieth century the Merchant Taylors' became less a professional and more a social organization and a very wealthy charitable benefactor, with about one thousand Freemen, three hundred and thirty Liverymen and just twenty invited members of Court. Angus's grandfather Howard, who died in 1927, had been the last practical tailor to be a Liveryman, but in 1990 Angus advanced from Freeman to Liveryman and, with Robert Bright, became the first practical tailor in sixty-three years to be 'in the Livery'.

By then it was clear that the next family generation in the business, the seventh in the line, was assured. Angus had two children, a son and a daughter, and from an early age his son Simon (born in 1968) showed a special interest in and flair for clothes and fashion. While still a schoolboy, Simon worked in the holidays for Salvatore Ferragamo, designer of shoes and fashion-wear (the actress Audrey Hepburn was one of Ferragamo's clients), and had already made up his mind that when he was adult he would work for Poole's.

Angus decided his son should have the best possible apprenticeship, so from 1986 Simon went through formal training at the London College of Fashion, a three-year course which taught him all aspects of practical tailoring. With this qualification he officially joined Henry Poole & Co, and for further experience was seconded to Taylor & Lodge, a famous textile mill in Huddersfield, Yorkshire. He spent four months there, watching and learning every part of the process from taking the incoming yarn to seeing it sent out as finished fabric, and while there, he – a 'soft young southerner' and a tailor, to boot – lodged with a former professional wrestler called Ted Fussey. Despite the differences in their backgrounds, they unexpectedly became firm friends, and in 2001 their lasting friendship was featured in the BBC Radio 4 series *Friends for Life*. It was also in 2001 that Simon advanced to the degree of Liveryman in the Merchant Taylors' Company, after serving his apprenticeship and having become a Freeman in 1989.

After Taylor & Lodge, he spent four months working in Paris, and on behalf of Poole's made the first of what would become many trips to Japan, visiting Nagoya, Osaka and Tokyo, meeting the company licensees and manufacturers and seeing the accessories marketed under the company name. In 1990 he joined the cutting room staff in Savile Row, but despite being a fully trained tailor and a good cutter, he

Simon Cundey. The seventh generation of the family to manage the business in nearly two hundred years.

preferred working with customers. He found he had a good memory for their individual likes and dislikes in the way their garments were made (a faculty which certainly eased his path with a few customers, doubtful about being served by such a young man) and he steadily built a strong personal client list, including among many others the film director John Hughes; Sir James Wolfensohn, president of the World Bank; and Fred Whittemore of Morgan Stanley. Another of his clients, Sir John Bourn, chairman of the National Audit Office, had an unusual family connection with Poole's: in 1900 his grandfather had been a coat-maker for the company.

Poole's in 1992 became a very early member of the Walpole Committee. Composed of representatives of many of Britain's most prestigious businesses and now simply called Walpole, this increasingly successful and influential body is dedicated to promoting British excellence abroad. Poole's has also begun to demonstrate a slightly unexpected skill at mounting large public static exhibitions (as distinct from fashion shows) of its products.

Its first experience in this line was an indirect one in 1994. As part of celebrations marking the thirtieth anniversary of the licensing agreement with Henry Poole & Co, Matsuzakaya staged an exhibition of Henry Poole clothing historic and modern. As well as many garments exhibited on tailor's dummies, the show included life-size waxworks lent by Madame Tussaud's of King Edward VII and Prime Minister Shigeru Yoshida, both appropriately dressed: the model of the prime

Merchant Taylors' Hall Exhibition 1995.
Henry Poole's stand shows some of the extraordinary range of their tailoring skills and their remarkable history.

minister wore an authentic Japanese outfit, and the model of the king wore a frock coat made by Poole's.

The next exhibition, the first to be created by Poole's, took place in the Merchant Taylors' Hall in 1995, and was followed in 1996–97 by a major display in the Textile and Costume department of the Victoria and Albert Museum (the V&A) in London. Opened by HRH The Princess Royal and presented in association with Coutts & Co, 'Dressing the Part: 190 Years of Savile Row Tailoring by Henry Poole' displayed thirty examples of suits, uniforms, parliamentary robes and other garments made by Poole's from 1870 to the 1990s, and gained extensive press coverage at home and abroad, especially in the USA.

The exhibition also led indirectly to the writing of this book, because one of the exhibits was described in the press as something 'thought to be Lord Nelson's uniform'. This puzzled the present writer, since Poole's was formed in 1806 and Nelson was killed in 1805. A telephone call established that the uniform was a hand-stitched replica researched and made by one of the company's apprentices, Keith Levett. With that query settled, the next was more unusual: Nelson married on the Caribbean island of Nevis, so would the company consider making another uniform, on behalf of the naval historical charity The 1805 Club, for presentation to the museum of the Nevis Historical and Conservation Society? Certainly, sir. The next query was still more unusual: given that it was for a charitable purpose, would the company consider making the uniform at no cost? Ah.

Nelson's uniform. On HMS Victory, Rear Admiral Peter Dunt RN (right) receives an accurate replica of Nelson's uniform made by Poole's apprentice Keith Levett (left) on behalf of The 1805 Club and for subsequent donation to the Nevis Historical and Conservation Society.

After consultation with Keith Levett, who agreed to give his time and skilled labour, Angus agreed that the firm would donate the materials, most of which he was able to source from the same manufacturers as in Nelson's day. Coat, waistcoat and breeches were made, the coat being entirely hand-sewn, and Lock's the hatters (who had made Nelson's hats) joined the project, making and donating a cocked hat made to Nelson's measurements, still proudly recorded in Lock's archives. Later, at a ceremony in Nelson's last and most famous flagship, HMS *Victory*, the magnificent uniform was presented to a member of the Nevis Society by Rear Admiral Peter Dunt, chief of staff to the Second Sea Lord; then in subsequent conversation, Angus outlined the history of his firm, and this book is the result.

Royal Visitor to number 15. In 1993 Angus Cundey shows HRH The Princess Royal some of Henry Poole's historic ledgers, which include many entries for the Royal Family.

Before the V&A exhibition, HRH The Princess Royal and Angus had already met, the first occasion being on 6 October 1993, when, as president of the British Knitting and Clothing Export Council (now UK Fashion Exports, of which Angus is a council member), Her Royal Highness paid an official visit to 15 Savile Row. The visit was intended to last an hour, but just as she was about to leave on time, she passed a display of the firm's historic ledgers, which naturally included many entries for the Royal Family. This interested her so much that despite the increasing restlessness of her staff, she stayed thirty minutes over schedule; and the same thing happened at the V&A. Her third meeting with Angus came on 13 January 1999, when Her Royal Highness presented him with the prestigious British Apparel Export Award; but on that occasion she managed to leave on time.

The company's French connections are of course very long standing and often at the highest levels: President Giscard d'Estaing was among its recent clients, his name and address unrevealed to the prying Customs chief. So was Edouard Balladur, Prime Minister from 1993 to 1995, who began buying regularly from Poole's in 1979. The more he rose up the political hierarchy, the more conspicuous was his English look: a French cartoon of 1994 showed British Prime Minister John

French Connection. When French Prime Minister Edouard Balladur stood for President on 'the "Believe in France"' platform, he gave up buying English suits from Henry Poole and lost in the first round!

Major admiring his suit. 'Your tailor is rich', said Major, to which Balladur replied, 'He is English!'

When Balladur announced in 1994 that he was going to run for the presidency, he soon became the favourite. However, London's *Evening Standard* reported that 'his advisors were fearful that wearing a Savile Row suit in his one and only campaign poster would give satirists a field day. Especially as the slogan reads: "Believe in France!"' The presidential candidate was persuaded to abandon Poole's, and when the elections began, the *Daily Telegraph* noted tersely: 'He lost in the first round.'

The *Standard* commented, 'If a man deserts his tailor, who will be next?', and although Angus declined to make any public connection between the two events, he did recollect the company's more gentlemanly attitude towards another French client, J. D. Jecquier, a member of the wartime Resistance. Shortly before the outbreak of war in 1939 Jecquier had ordered a suit. He survived to come and collect it in 1946, and was delighted to be charged only the 1939 price.

Moving back across the Atlantic to American customers, in 1996 Angus's son Simon took charge of all fittings and business in the USA, and soon acquired three high-status corporate clients. Four members of the Old Elm Golf Club at Lake Forest, Chicago, were keen customers and put Henry Poole's name forward as the potential maker of club jackets. The tender was satisfactory, the company was taken on, and word began to get around that Old Elm jackets were something really special. Prompted by reading an article in the *Wall Street Journal*, a committee member at the Augusta National Golf Club, who was also a Poole's customer, proposed that the club should invite Poole's to tender there too. Augusta, steeped in tradition, required a very particular look and cut and an absolutely precise shade of green, all of which was well within Poole's capabilities, and at the company's presentation Jack Stephens, club chairman at the time, personally approved the choice of fabric. Watch any Masters' championship at Augusta and you will see Poole's jackets – with the exception of the jacket presented to the champion on the day, since the winner's identity is obviously unknown beforehand. But Poole's supply the cloth for the champion's jacket too.

Third of these new corporate clients was the Lyford Cay Club, a private resort club at Nassau in the Bahamas. Once again the proposal that Poole's should tailor for the club came from a member who was a customer of the firm, and with its wealthy members from all over the world, Lyford Cay is like Poole's world-wide market concentrated in miniature form in one place.

Augusta's green cloth. Henry Poole & Co supplies the Augusta National Golf Club, home of the US Masters Tournament, with its world-famous green cloth and also makes many of the members' jackets. Senior cutter Jim Cottrell stands in front of the Clubhouse.

Angus once had the audacity to ask a personal customer – a very successful and extremely busy man – what it was that he particularly liked about Poole's and its tailoring. The customer's answer was revealing: it was not only the cut, the quality and the style that appealed, but the good use of time. The fact that an order took a while to be completed was irrelevant; what was important was that because the staff knew him so well, he could come to 15 Savile Row and, with their expert advice, choose fifteen shirts, five ties and the fabrics for four suits inside twenty minutes. He would then call in at the New York Intercontinental Hotel for a first fitting – again, twenty minutes. Then he would return to Savile Row for his second fitting – another twenty minutes – and in due course the clothes would be delivered. It was

143

"We make your coachmen's liveries, Your Majesty".
When HM The Queen met her Royal Warrant Holders,
Simon Cundey (right), with his father Angus in the
background, had the honour of explaining his company's
long-standing royal connections.

Royal Cypher for a postillion's coat.

quick, simple, enjoyable and effective. The alternative would be spend an entire Saturday going around a department store, something he detested, and waste time buying clothes which were much less well-made, much less comfortable, and in which he would feel much less well dressed. By coming to Poole's instead, he could confidently buy his entire main wardrobe for the year in a single hour.

Angus once again gave of his own time in 2000. Feeling he should return something to the trade in which he had made his life, he undertook the role of president of the Master Tailors' Benevolent Association (as his grandfather and its co-founder Howard had been for several years), and on 20 March 2002, with Poole's as a prominent member of the Royal Warrant Holders' Association, he and his son Simon had the pleasure and honour of being presented to HM Queen Elizabeth II. This was the first occasion on which the monarch had taken lunch with her tradesmen, and the Association's official history remarks that Poole's 'must be among the all-time record holders for the number of Warrants held.' From its first, the Imperial Warrant of Napoleon III, to its most recent, the Royal Warrant as suppliers of Livery to Her Majesty, it certainly would be hard to beat the company's total of forty.

Angus and Keith Levett followed this in the summer of 2002 with another remarkable pair of gifts, this time to the Merchant Taylors' Company. The Company's origins go back to an unknown date before the year 1300. In 1327 it received its first Royal Charter, and in 1481 its first coat of arms. Keith had discovered that two large banners depicting these used to hang in its majestic Hall. One showed the Company's coat of arms before the Reformation of the Church in 1586 (that is, its Catholic arms) and the other, its subsequent Protestant arms. Both banners had long vanished, but their ornate designs were known, and Angus and Keith decided to commission replacement banners. Keith donated the pre-Reformation banner, Henry Poole's the post-Reformation one, and both were presented and unveiled on Wednesday 29 May 2002.

Shortly afterwards, at the time of his sixty-fifth birthday, Angus took the opportunity of semi-retirement and began coming into the shop three days a week. Pondering Poole's future, he was reasonably optimistic. From long experience he had complete confidence in its entire staff. Every man and woman was expert in their tasks, or if they were not yet expert (a new trainee cutter had been taken on) they showed great promise and, with Poole's training, would become expert. The training of young people as the bespoke tailors of the future was still one of his great preoccupations, and he was encouraged by the fact that as well as young men, there were growing numbers of young women applicants. As the *Evening Standard* wrote,

> *With its air of confident, discreet masculinity and ancient traditions, Savile Row may seem no place for a young woman to carve out a career. But in the cutting rooms of the most famous tailoring street in the world, young women are painstakingly learning the trade…*

Poole's at the time employed three women in their workshops – 'not the first,' the *Standard* continued, 'but they are the generation that can make their mark.' Angus now found himself in the unaccustomed position of having to turn away more and more talented young people, simply because of space restrictions. In one way it was very welcome news that so many of the rising generation wished to join the trade and actively sought out Poole's first and foremost, but he did not enjoy the knowledge that they would probably be snapped up by competitors and their nascent skills lost to Poole's.

Presentation to Merchant Taylors' Company. In 2002, Henry Poole and Keith Levett commissioned replica banners of the Merchant Taylors' original pre- and post-Reformation coats of arms. Left to right: Philip Parker; the Master, Alderman D W Brewer; Angus Cundey; Keith Levett; the Clerk, David Peck.

One reason for the increasing numbers of applicants was an improved (though from the trade's view still imperfect) structuring of English educational possibilities. Another was the increasing recognition among creative young people that in bespoke tailoring, the sweat-shop days were long gone, and that with all the proper benefits of a modern industry (paid sick leave, paid holiday entitlement, proper pensions and so on), there were more secure long-term benefits – not to mention job satisfaction – in Savile Row than in many other more superficially attractive options.

This recognition and Angus's personal convictions were underlined by a series of events, starting when he was interviewed by Japanese television on the subject of 'dress-down Friday'. This was not an entirely new concept: a hundred years and more previously, it had been quite acceptable for gentlemen working in the City to come to the office on Fridays clad in country brown, because it was understood that at the end of the working week, one would go 'down to the country'. But 'dress-down Friday', introduced into the UK by the accountancy firm Arthur Andersen, was different in concept and owed nothing to the historical norms.

Investigating this, the Japanese television crew came to Angus fresh from an interview with an Arthur Andersen executive whose Friday office-wear had been a

Henry Poole staff in 2002 pose outside 15 Savile Row.

red sweater and blue jeans. Was this, they asked Angus, the death of the suit? What effect would it have on his business? His answer was direct: 'I think it more likely that it will affect Arthur Andersen', and he added at the interview's end, 'I wouldn't let them anywhere near *my* money.'

The highly dramatic next step was that in 2001–2002, as a combined result of allegedly corrupt management practices and inadequate or incompetent financial auditing, the huge American energy company Enron – audited by Arthur Andersen – collapsed, triggering a wave of worldwide financial insecurity as faith in US economic probity came under serious doubt; and it is not a silly thing to link such great items as globally influential financial probity with such apparently minor items as dress. Dress affects the way the wearer is viewed, and more importantly is an indicator of how the wearer views himself or herself in relation to the situation. This is why formal and informal clothing exists – in order to denote whatever role one might be performing. To adopt an inappropriate style denotes an inappropriate way of thinking. Putting it simply, no good chief executive officer would even think of wearing the apron of a barbecue chef in the office, and when cooking at the family barbecue the same individual would not dream of wearing his – or her – Savile Row suit.

Shortly afterwards, and as a very satisfying coda to his years working full-time for Henry Poole & Co, Angus received a completely unexpected professional accolade, once again involving Japanese media – this time, a leading magazine which invited him to be interviewed with Sir Paul Smith, whom many people have described as the greatest designer of men's fashion wear not only in the twentieth century but also in the opening years of the twenty-first. Perhaps the journalist expected to be able to make a story about a clash between the two men, the one a top traditional tailor and the other a top modern designer; but their meeting at Sir Paul's shop in Floral Street, London, was the very opposite of a clash. Angus went to it happily, because he admired Sir Paul both for his design skills and his tremendous business acumen; and to his great pleasure he discovered this respect was fully reciprocated. Sir Paul, while showing him round the Floral Street shop, not only praised Savile Row in general but also made clear his very high opinion of Poole's in particular – its history and traditions, its discreet ways, and above all the beautiful quality of its hand-sewn tailoring.

A little more research could have shown the journalist that his expectations had been wrong. Angus had already said about Poole's, 'Traditional? I'm not against it. Classic? I don't mind being thought of in that way. But old-fashioned? Never.' He and his company had responded most constructively to Tommy Nutter's innovations; why should they not respond equally constructively to the modernist Sir Paul? If there was a surprise in the meeting between Angus and Sir Paul, it was not the warmth of Angus's view, but of Sir Paul's response and their immediate professional and personal liking and esteem. So the journalist did not get the story he expected, a clash between these representatives of tradition and modernity; but instead he gained a very much better story of the rapport between two men who were seemingly at opposite ends of the tailoring spectrum.

Over the coming two or three decades, the biggest challenge for Savile Row as a whole is to keep both its manufacturing and the training of the next generation of Britain's bespoke tailors within the Row and its generic area. Ridley may have been theoretically right in saying the manufacture could take place elsewhere, but hardly any outworkers take on apprentices, and without apprentices the skills will die. Consequently the view within the traditional Row is that workshops *there*, not elsewhere, are indispensable for the proper training of apprentices.

For Poole's especially, its treasured national and international clientele are also essential, as are the happy links with Matsuzakaya and Chikuma in Japan; and with an eye to more new markets, links for the supply of bespoke tailoring in China are being explored.

And so we reach the end of this narrative; but it is easier to conclude the history of an institution that is dead and gone than of one which is still vibrant and alive, and there is no easy ending to this book – the story of Henry Poole & Co, the making of a legend – because, after all the real triumphs of professional skill and despite the sometimes tragic and all too human results of financial trust, the story is unfinished.

Nearly two centuries on from its beginning, there have been several times when anyone outside the family business might reasonably have expected it to collapse. First and most notable was the dire situation after the death of Henry Poole, but there was also the time following the deaths of Howard and Mabel, and the consequent double death duties borne by Sam and Hugh; there was the time when, following poor advice, the brothers sold their freeholds; and there was the time when out-of-date accounting methods seemed to show the company was insolvent. Yet this unique firm – a company owned and managed since its beginning by the same family, and providing the very highest quality product to an elite and discerning clientele – still survives. This is probably because its main objective has

Savile Row bespoke meets High Street retail. Angus Cundey (left) and outstanding High Street designer Sir Paul Smith find much in common in their search for tailoring excellence.

never been the pursuit of wealth. A curious journalist once asked Angus if he, as tailor to so many of the wealthy and powerful, was himself rich. His answer, 'worthy of a gentleman', was

> *I have job satisfaction. We don't pay ourselves very much. But we are very privileged to be able to meet charming, clever people we all respect.*

He could have added that with this attitude, he and his colleagues also enjoyed the pleasure of constantly developing their own creative skills to the top most level of their art, and in doing so had provided employment to many, and style leadership to many more; but to say so much might have been an unnecessary elaboration. The style lies in discretion, not in show.

So let us conclude this book – an interim report of an active business, not its final record – with two echoes from the past designed to presage the future. First is part of a lively advertisement published in 1872 by a Poole's cutter who had emigrated to Australia:

PRIZE TAILORING ESTABLISHMENT.

> *J.A. Allan, Military Tailor and Habit Maker (From Poole's, Saville-row, London), Promises his Customers that the Garment he makes for them* SHALL FIT *and not merely* LAY UPON THEIR LIMBS. *…In fact, the Advertiser can promise safely that Gentlemen entrusting themselves to his care will be* DRESSED AS GENTLEMEN, *and will never be mistaken for anything else, and this satisfactory and desirable result can be achieved at as little cost as the* INEXPERIENCED BOTCHERS *entail upon their misguided Customers.*

No changes there, then; botchers have never had a place at Poole's, and the long life of a Henry Poole garment easily offsets its cost.

Next let us take a verse published shortly after the death of Henry Poole himself. Though composed for amusement it is a good epigraph on that historic man and his times, and contains a signpost to the future of the firm which bears his name:

Yes, Poole's my tailor. Poole! You know!
Who makes the Prince of Wales's things.
He's tailor (as his billheads show)
To half the emperors and kings.
An introduction is required
At Poole's, before they'll take your trade.
No common people are desired,
However promptly bills are paid.
Yet my bill shows, 'mongst other things,
'Discount for cash – fifteen per cent.'
Oh, can it be that, sometimes kings
Are – shall we call it 'negligent'?
Some several things about this bill
Lead me to ponder and to muse;
Such names – the Emperor of Brazil,
The Emperor of the French – they use.
Though once these names great lustre shed,
Deposed, deceased, forgot are they;
And Poole himself, I'm told, is dead,
But his name lives and holds its sway.

So it does, and the legendary name of Henry Poole & Co is still what it has been for nearly two hundred years: the arbiter not of passing fashion, but of supreme English style for discerning ladies and gentlemen in the world of bespoke tailoring. James Poole started it in his steady, modest but ambitious way; in the second generation his son Henry created the legend; and under their cousins the Cundeys – Samuel as the third generation, Howard the fourth, Sam and Hugh the fifth, Angus the sixth, and now Simon as the seventh of the line – the legend lives on.

A simplified Family Tree of the Pooles and Cundeys
most closely associated with Henry Poole's, with heads of the firm in bold.
(Certain antecedents of James Poole are listed in Chapter 1.)

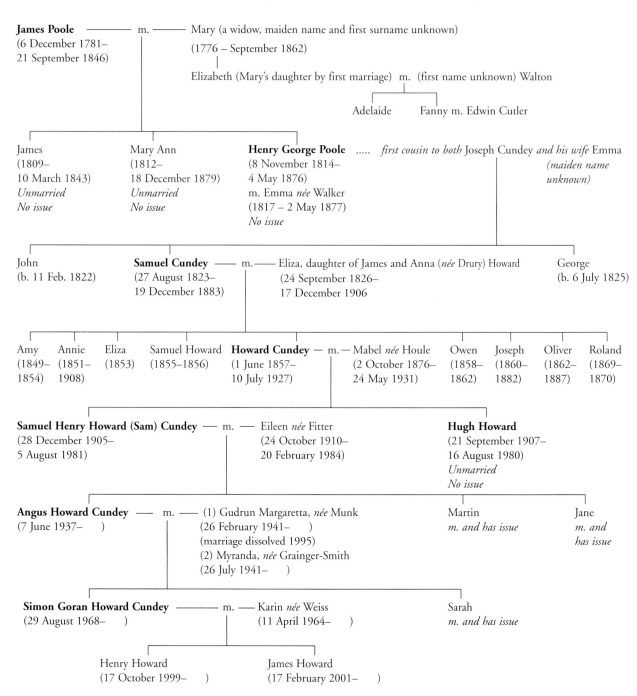

James Poole ——— m. ——— Mary (a widow, maiden name and first surname unknown)
(6 December 1781–
21 September 1846) (1776 – September 1862)

Elizabeth (Mary's daughter by first marriage) m. (first name unknown) Walton

Adelaide   Fanny m. Edwin Cutler

James   Mary Ann   **Henry George Poole** ..... *first cousin to both* Joseph Cundey *and his wife* Emma
(1809–   (1812–   (8 November 1814–   *(maiden name*
10 March 1843)   18 December 1879)   4 May 1876)   *unknown)*
Unmarried   *Unmarried*   m. Emma *née* Walker
No issue   *No issue*   (1817 – 2 May 1877)
                    No issue

John   **Samuel Cundey** ——— m. ——— Eliza, daughter of James and Anna (*née* Drury) Howard   George
(b. 11 Feb. 1822)   (27 August 1823–   (24 September 1826–   (b. 6 July 1825)
        19 December 1883)   17 December 1906

Amy   Annie   Eliza   Samuel Howard   **Howard Cundey** — m. — Mabel *née* Houle   Owen   Joseph   Oliver   Roland
(1849–   (1851–   (1853)   (1855–1856)   (1 June 1857–   (2 October 1876–   (1858–   (1860–   (1862–   (1869–
1854)   1908)   10 July 1927)   24 May 1931)   1862)   1882)   1887)   1870)

Samuel Henry Howard (Sam) Cundey — m. — Eileen *née* Fitter   **Hugh Howard**
(28 December 1905–   (24 October 1910–   (21 September 1907–
5 August 1981)   20 February 1984)   16 August 1980)
                    Unmarried
                    No issue

Angus Howard Cundey — m. — (1) Gudrun Margaretta, *née* Munk   Martin   Jane
(7 June 1937–   )   (26 February 1941–   )   *m. and has issue*   *m. and*
            (marriage dissolved 1995)   *has issue*
            (2) Myranda, *née* Grainger-Smith
            (26 July 1941–   )

Simon Goran Howard Cundey ——— m. — Karin *née* Weiss   Sarah
(29 August 1968–   )   (11 April 1964–   )   *m. and has issue*

Henry Howard   James Howard
(17 October 1999–   )   (17 February 2001–   )

Poole's Warrants of Appointment

HIM The Emperor Napoleon III	1858
HRH The Prince of Wales	1863
HRH The Duke of Edinburgh	1868
HRH The Crown Prince of Prussia	1868
HM Queen Victoria	1869
HM The King of the Belgians	1869
HRH The Crown Prince of Denmark	1869
HRH The Prince of Teck	1870
HRH Prince Christian of Schleswig-Holstein	1870
The Khedive of Egypt	1870
HRH Prince Oscar of Sweden and Norway	1871
HM King Amadeus I of Spain	1871
HRH Prince Louis of Hesse	1871
HRH Crown Prince Alexander of Russia	1874
HIM The Emperor Pedro II of Brazil	1874
HIM Tsar Alexander II of Russia	1875
HM The King of the Hellenes	1877
HRH The Crown Prince of Austria	1878
HM King Umberto I of Italy	1879
HIM Emperor Wilhelm I of Germany	*
HIM Tsar Alexander III of Russia	1881
HG The Duke of Genoa	1891
HG Friedrich, Grossherzog of Baden	1891
HG The Duke of Aosta	1892
HRH Prince Emanuel of Savoie	1892
HIM The Shah of Persia	*
HM The King of Denmark	1893
HM King Edward VII	1902
HRH Prince Albrecht of Prussia	1903
HH The Maharajah Gaekwar of Baroda	1905
HIM The Shah of Persia	1906
The Khedive of Egypt	1910
HM Queen Alexandra	1911
HRH The Prince of Wales	1922
The Imperial Household of Japan	1923
HM King George V	1928
HM The King of the Bulgarians	1936
HM King George VI	1940
HIM Emperor Haile Selassie	1959
HM Queen Elizabeth II	1976

* Poole's records show that these Warrants were issued, but not the dates of issue.

Index